HAL LEONARD KEYBOARD STYLE SERIES

SMOOTH JAZZ PIANO

THE COMPLETE GUIDE WITH AUDIO!

PLAYBACK+

Speed • Pitch • Balance • Loop

To access audio visit:
www.halleonard.com/mylibrary

2710-4982-3891-6760

BY MARK HARRISON

ISBN 978-0-634-07394-6

HAL•LEONARD®
CORPORATION

7777 W. BLUEMOUND RD. P.O. BOX 13819 MILWAUKEE, WI 53213

T0055422

In Australia Contact:
Hal Leonard Australia Pty. Ltd.
22 Taunton Drive P.O. Box 5130
Cheltenham East, 3192 Victoria, Australia
Email: ausadmin@halleonard.com

Visit Hal Leonard Online at **www.halleonard.com**

INTRODUCTION

Welcome to *Smooth Jazz Piano*. If you're interested in playing today's smooth jazz on the piano, but were never quite sure how, then you've come to the right place! Whatever your playing level, this book will help you sound more authentic in your smooth jazz stylings.

After reviewing some essential chords and scales, we'll dig into the voicing techniques and rhythmic patterns that are vital for the smooth jazz pianist. We'll focus on "comping" (accompaniment) grooves as well as playing melodies and solos. This will help you to create your own piano parts on a variety of smooth jazz tunes and progressions!

In the process we'll also see how smooth jazz styles evolved by combining jazz melodies and harmonies with pop/R&B rhythms and instrumentation. We'll spotlight the important smooth jazz pianists and keyboardists and learn how to incorporate their vocabulary into our own music.

Several tunes in various smooth jazz styles are included in the "Style File" chapter at the end of the book. Jam with the rhythm section on these tunes using the play-along audio—this is a great way to develop your piano chops within these different grooves.

Good luck with your smooth jazz piano!

—*Mark Harrison*

About the Audio

On the accompanying audio, you'll find demonstrations of most of the music examples in the book. The solo piano tracks feature the left-hand part on the left channel, and the right-hand part on the right channel, for easy "hands separate" practice. The full band tracks feature the rhythm section on the left channel and the piano on the right channel, so that you can play along with the band. Also, the Chapter 5 examples (creating melodies and solos) each have an extra track with the right-hand part on the right channel, and the left-hand part and the rhythm section all on the left channel, if you need to practice just the right-hand part along with the band. This is all designed to give you maximum flexibility when practicing! Please see the individual chapters for specific information on the audio tracks and how to use them.

About the Author

Mark Harrison is a *Keyboard Magazine* columnist and an educational author whose books are used by thousands of musicians worldwide. His TV credits include *Saturday Night Live, American Justice, Celebrity Profiles,* and many other shows and commercials. As a working keyboardist in the Los Angeles area, Mark performs regularly with the top-flight Steely Dan tribute band Doctor Wu, as well as the critically acclaimed Mark Harrison Quintet. He has also shared the stage with top musicians such as John Molo (Bruce Hornsby band) and Jimmy Haslip (Yellowjackets), and is currently co-writing an R&B/pop project with the Grammy-winning songwriter Ron Dunbar. For further information on Mark's musical activities and education products, please visit *www.harrisonmusic.com.*

CONTENTS

Chapter 1
WHAT IS SMOOTH JAZZ?

Smooth jazz is an American music style which emerged in the 1980s, and is descended from the fusion of jazz and rock styles that first occurred in the 1960s. It is a mostly instrumental style, in which piano and keyboards play a central role. In order to understand the characteristics of smooth jazz and its relationship to other jazz styles, we need to trace some of the evolutionary steps that jazz has taken from the 1960s up until the present.

Jazz-Rock Fusion

In the 1960s, jazz musicians began combining the new rock rhythms and instrumentation with jazz harmony and improvisation, thus giving birth to the term "fusion." Miles Davis is widely regarded as the foremost innovator in this area, and his seminal fusion album *Bitches Brew* is an all-time classic that is credited with launching the jazz-rock era. Many great players from the various Miles Davis lineups went on to launch successful jazz and fusion careers, creating what we might call the first wave of fusion artists that emerged in the 1970s. Notable pianists/keyboardists among this first wave include:

* Herbie Hancock, who formed his own sextet after leaving Miles Davis, and who has since played most jazz styles from bebop to hard-core funk/R&B.

* Chick Corea, who ran the gamut from Brazilian jazz to rock with his band Return To Forever, and then switched effortlessly between energetic jazz-funk (with his Elektric Band) and more traditional swing and bebop (with his Akoustic Band).

* Joe Zawinul, whose electric piano was a key component of Miles's sound. Together with saxophonist Wayne Shorter, he formed the band Weather Report, who created some of the most important fusion music of the 1970s. Zawinul is still going strong into this millennium with the Zawinul Syndicate.

Other famous Miles Davis alumni include the drummer Tony Williams, who formed the Jimi Hendrix-influenced band Lifetime (with the great keyboardist Alan Pasqua), and guitarist John McLaughlin, who formed the high-volume Mahavishnu Orchestra, which crossed over very successfully to rock audiences.

Contemporary Jazz

In the 1980s, the second wave of electric-oriented jazz groups began to emerge. These artists were classified in the new "contemporary jazz" category. As we will see, this category began to incorporate various sub-styles (including smooth jazz). Artists in this second wave included a heavy dose of R&B in their jazz improvisations and were arguably less rhythmically freewheeling than their first wave predecessors, instead favoring more accessible grooves. Noted artists in this second wave include:

* Yellowjackets, including pianist/keyboardist Russell Ferrante. A uniquely creative and thoughtful group, their music shows a deep respect for traditional jazz and bebop, while incorporating funk, blues, gospel, and world music elements to create cutting-edge contemporary jazz.

* Spyro Gyra, including pianist/keyboardist Tom Schuman. This popular group is noted for adding Latin rhythms to its jazz harmony and improvisations.

* Saxophonists David Sanborn and Grover Washington Jr., who epitomize the R&B-flavored improvisation and rhythmic stylings associated with many contemporary jazz artists.

4

From the mid-1980s into the 1990s, contemporary jazz started to become a catchall category incorporating various jazz sub-styles. Unfortunately these labels are not very precise, and there may be some overlap between sub-styles to some extent. These various sub-styles can be described as follows.

Jazz-Funk or "Crossover" Jazz

This has an emphasis on R&B/funk rhythms, and the melodies and improvisation are influenced by the blues and R&B. Noted artists in this style are David Sanborn, Grover Washington Jr., and Richard Elliott.

Pop-Jazz or "Jazzy Pop"

This has an emphasis on accessible and commercial melodies, with simpler harmonies and rhythms. There may be little or no improvisation (a yardstick used by some critics when deciding whether a style is "jazz" or not). Perhaps the most famous artist in this category is the saxophonist Kenny G (who, when previously known as Kenny Gorelick, played high-octane fusion with the Jeff Lorber band).

Smooth Jazz

This style has an emphasis on mellow rhythmic grooves and polished production. Smooth jazz artists will often use some limited (compared to mainstream jazz or fusion) chord alterations and improvisation, within a light R&B or funk framework. The melodies are typically sparse and/or repetitive, using blues or penta-tonic scales. Both acoustic and electric sounds are used, with an avoidance of harsh textures. Noted artists in this style include keyboardists Joe Sample (formerly of the Crusaders), Brian Culbertson, Gregg Karukas, Jeff Lorber (his later period), David Benoit and Bob James (from the band Fourplay), and saxophonists Dave Koz and Boney James.

New Age Jazz

This has an emphasis on calming and soothing sounds, with gently flowing rhythms rather than energetic grooves. It functions as both listening music and background music. Any improvisation used is normally of lower intensity and applied within gradually changing harmonies. Sounds used can either be acoustic or highly processed and electronic. There are little or no blues and R&B influences. Most new age music is in fact outside of the realm of jazz, but some artists (notably Acoustic Alchemy and keyboardist Keiko Matsui) create interesting blends of new age and jazz elements. Also, the seminal new age pianist George Winston developed his style by distilling some of Keith Jarrett's jazz improvisations into a much more basic form.

Even though an artist may produce music that falls into a category mentioned above, it does not mean that the artist's entire output belongs in the same category. For example, jazz icons such as guitarist Pat Metheny and pianist David Benoit have produced tunes that could be called New Age Jazz, even though this category would certainly not apply to their work as a whole. Keyboardist Jeff Lorber's more recent output would be considered smooth jazz, even though his older work was more high-energy jazz fusion. Radio stations billing themselves as "smooth jazz" (i.e. KTWV in Los Angeles) may actually have playlists encompassing any or all of the above styles, often adding some R&B/pop to the mix as well.

Chapter 2

SCALES and CHORDS

Major scales and modes

First, we'll look at the **major scale**, which is the fundamental basis of harmony in most contemporary music styles. I recommend that you think of this scale in terms of the intervals it contains—whole step, whole step, half step, whole step, whole step, whole step, half step—as this most closely parallels how the ear relates to the scale. Here is the C major scale, showing these intervals:

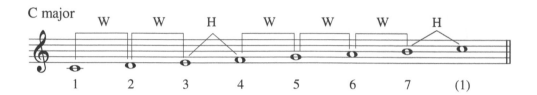

This major scale pattern can be applied to any root note. Here for your reference are all of the major scales. After C major, the next seven scales contain flats, i.e. F major has one flat, B♭ major has two flats, and so on. The next seven scales contain sharps, i.e. G major has one sharp; D major has two sharps, and so on.

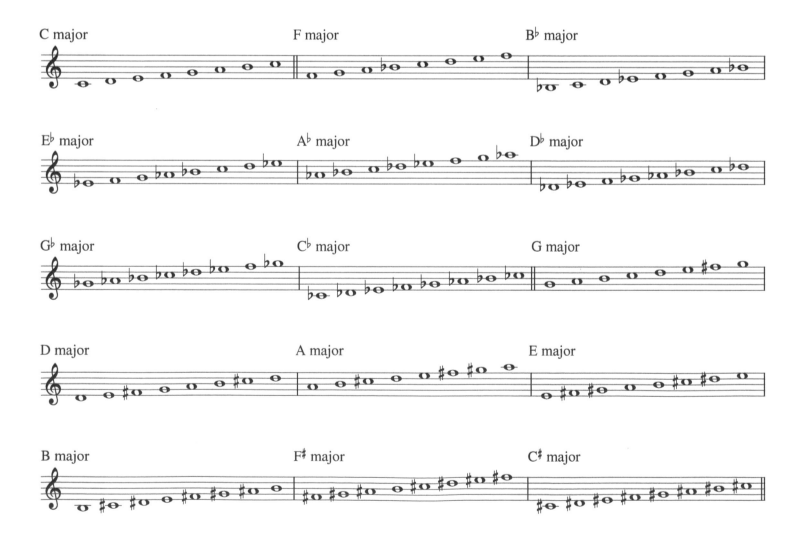

In this book, we'll work with music examples in different major and minor keys. For example, a tune will be "in the key of C major" if the note C is heard as the tonic or "home base," and if the notes used are within the C major scale (except for any sharped or flatted notes occurring in the music). Similarly, a tune will be "in the key of A minor" if the note A is heard as the tonic or "home base," and if the notes used are within an A minor scale (again except for any sharped or flatted notes). Later in this chapter, we'll learn more about minor scales.

A **key signature** is a group of flats or sharps at the beginning of the music that lets you know which key you are in. Each key signature works for both a **major** and a **minor** key, which are considered relative to one another. The first key signature shown below (no sharps and no flats) works for both the keys of C major and A minor. To find out which minor key shares the same key signature as a major key, we can count up to the 6th degree of the corresponding major scale. In the first example, the 6th degree of a C major scale is the note A, so the keys of C major and A minor are relative to one another and share the same key signature.

Here for your reference are all of the major and minor key signatures:

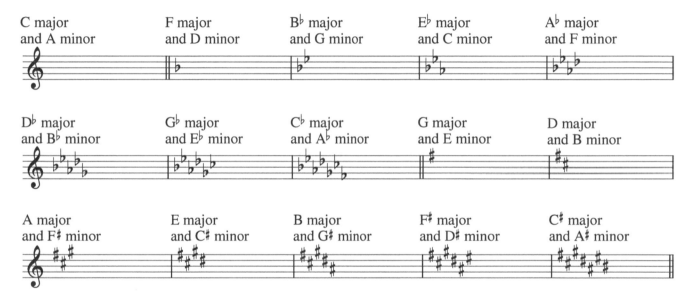

A **mode** or modal scale is created when we start a major scale on another scale degree than the original root. An example of this is the **Dorian** mode, created when the major scale is started on the 2nd degree. In the following example, a C major scale is displaced to create a D Dorian mode:

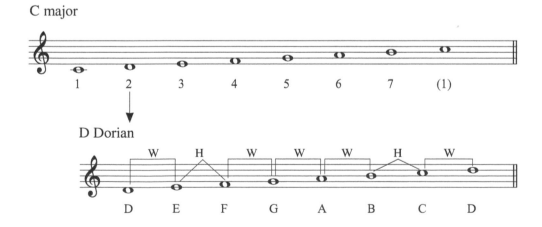

If you compare the two scales above, you'll see that the notes are the same; they just begin (and end) at different points—C major begins and ends on C, while D Dorian begins and ends on D. Each scale has a different implied tonic (root), and therefore a different pattern of whole and half steps from one note to the next, resulting in a different overall sound.

An alternative way to derive the Dorian mode is to build it from its own root, following the step pattern shown in the previous staff. When seen this way, the Dorian mode contains the same notes as a major scale, with a flatted 3rd and 7th (1–2–♭3–4–5–6–♭7).

The Dorian mode has a "minor" sound, due to the minor 3rd interval between the tonic and 3rd degree (in this case from D to F), and is widely used as a scale source for minor chords, melodies, and solos in smooth jazz styles. You should make it a goal to learn all of the Dorian modes, as shown in the following example. Each of these starts on the 2nd degree of a previously shown major scale:

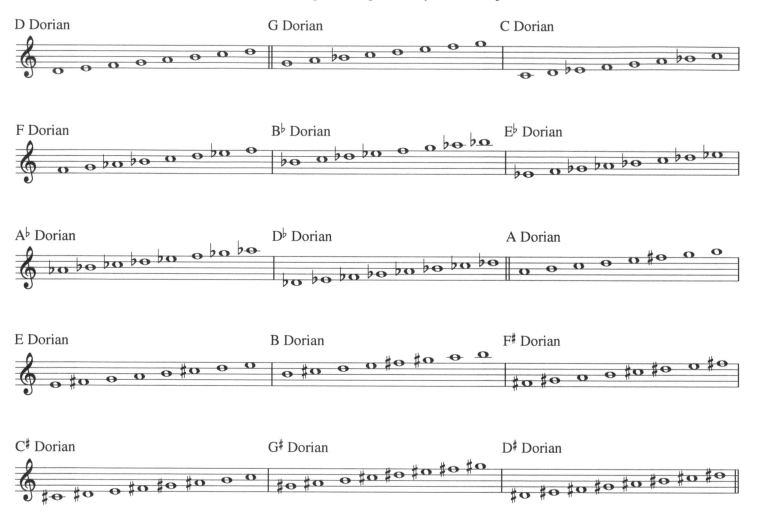

Another useful mode in smooth jazz styles is the **Mixolydian** mode, created when the major scale is displaced to start on the 5th degree. In the following example, a C major scale is displaced to create a G Mixolydian mode:

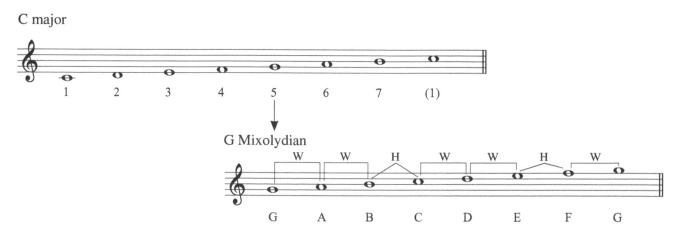

You can also think of the Mixolydian mode as a major scale with a flatted 7th (1–2–3–4–5–6–♭7). The Mixolydian mode is the basic scale source for a **dominant seventh chord** (more about these shortly) and is therefore very useful when creating melodies and solos over dominant harmonies.

Pentatonic and blues scales

The **major pentatonic** scale (also known as the pentatonic scale) is a five-note scale widely used in smooth jazz, as well as in rock and new age styles. It can be derived from the major scale by removing the 4th and 7th degrees:

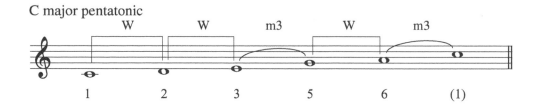

Note that from bottom to top, this scale now contains the following intervals: whole step, whole step, minor 3rd, whole step, minor 3rd. Listen for the unique open sound this scale creates. You should make it a goal to learn the pentatonic scale in all keys. Derive them by removing the 4th and 7th degrees of the major scale.

The **minor pentatonic** scale (a.k.a. blues pentatonic) can be derived from the major pentatonic scale. For example, if we start the C major pentatonic scale on the note A (which is the relative minor of C), we create an A minor pentatonic scale, as follows:

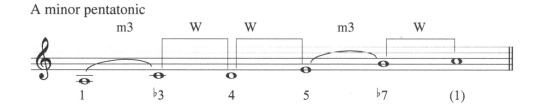

Note that from bottom to top, this scale now contains the following intervals: minor 3rd, whole-step, whole-step, minor 3rd, whole-step.

Finally, the **blues scale** can be derived by adding one note, the ♯4/♭5, to the minor pentatonic scale. For example, if we take the A minor pentatonic scale and add the "connecting tone" D♯ between the notes D and E, we create an A blues scale, as follows:

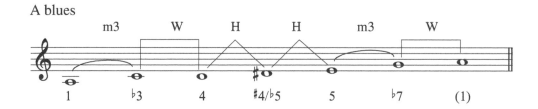

The blues scale is a signature sound in smooth jazz melodies and solos, so you should make it a goal to learn it in all keys. Practice all twelve minor pentatonic scales and add the sharp 4th (or flat 5th as many players prefer to think of it) to each, listening for the bluesy quality of the scale and this note in particular.

Natural and melodic minor scales

Next, we'll take a look at two of the **minor scales** that are prominent in smooth jazz. If we stay within a minor key without using any extra accidentals (sharps or flats) in the music, we are using a **natural minor** scale. Again, it is good to think of this scale in terms of the intervals it contains. Here is the C natural minor scale, showing its intervals:

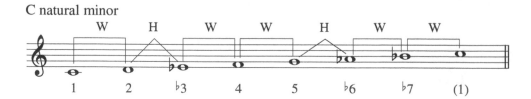

You can also think of natural minor as a major scale with a flatted 3rd, 6th, and 7th (1–2–♭3–4–5–♭6–♭7). Note that this scale is also equivalent to the sixth mode of a major scale (known as the **Aeolian** mode). For example, if we were to play an E♭ major scale, starting and ending on the 6th degree, the C Aeolian mode would be created.

The natural minor scale is the most commonly used source for melodies and chords in minor key applications, not only in smooth jazz but also in mainstream pop, rock, and R&B styles. Next we will look at the **melodic minor scale**, which is often used when improvising over altered harmonies in jazz styles. Here is the C melodic minor scale, again showing the internal intervals:

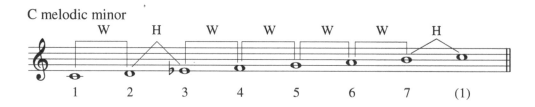

You can also think of the melodic minor scale as a major scale with a flatted 3rd (1–2–♭3–4–5–6–7). Classical or traditional theory often distinguishes between different ascending and descending forms of this scale; however, this distinction is not used for contemporary applications. In Chapter 5 we will see how these minor scales are used when creating melodies and solos in smooth jazz styles.

Triads

There are four main types of triad (3-part chord) in common usage: **major**, **minor**, **augmented**, and **diminished**. The following example shows all of these triads, built from the root C:

Note that these triads are formed by building the following **intervals** above the root note:

Major triad:	Major 3rd and perfect 5th (1–3–5)
Minor triad:	Minor 3rd and perfect 5th (1–♭3–5)
Augmented triad:	Major 3rd and augmented 5th (1–3–♯5)
Diminished triad:	Minor 3rd and diminished 5th (1–♭3–♭5)

If we construct triads from each degree of the major scale and stay within the restrictions of the scale, we create **diatonic** triads. "Diatonic" means the notes are drawn from the major scale only. Here are the diatonic triads found within the C major scale:

Relating the above triads to the four main triad types, note that **major** triads are built from the 1st, 4th, and 5th major scale degrees, minor triads are built from the 2nd, 3rd, and 6th scale degrees, and a **diminished** triad is built from the 7th scale degree. (The augmented triad does not occur anywhere in the diatonic series).

major	minor	minor	major	major	minor	diminished
I	ii	iii	IV	V	vi	vii°

Simpler smooth jazz and new age jazz tunes (as well as a lot of commercial pop, rock, and R&B) use diatonic triad chord progressions, so you should strive to learn these in as many keys as possible.

Seventh (four-part) chords and alterations

The term "seventh chord" is sometimes used to describe four-part chords in which the highest note or extension is the 7th. The four-part chords most commonly used in smooth jazz are the **major seventh**, **minor seventh**, **dominant seventh**, and **suspended dominant seventh** chords. The following example shows these four-part chords, built from the root C:

Note that these chords are formed by building the following intervals above the root note:

Major 7th chord:	Major 3rd, perfect 5th, and major 7th (1–3–5–7)
Minor 7th chord:	Minor 3rd, perfect 5th, and minor 7th (1–♭3–5–♭7)
Dominant 7th chord:	Major 3rd, perfect 5th, and minor 7th (1–3–5–♭7)
Suspended Dominant 7th chord:	Perfect 4th, perfect 5th, and minor 7th (1–4–5–♭7)

It is also possible to **alter** the major, minor, and dominant 7th chords by flatting or sharping the 5th of the chord by one half step. Of these possibilities, the following four-part altered chords are the most useful in smooth jazz styles:

Each of these chords is an alteration of one of the previous four-part chords:

- Cmaj7♭5 and Cmaj7♯5 can be derived by altering the 5th of the major 7th chord.
- Cm7♭5 can be derived by flatting the 5th of the minor 7th chord.
- C+7 can be derived by sharping the 5th of the dominant 7th chord.

Of course these altered chords can also be formed by building intervals above the root:

Major 7th ♭5 chord:	Major 3rd, diminished 5th, and major 7th (1–3–♭5–7)
Major 7th ♯5 chord:	Major 3rd, augmented 5th, and major 7th (1–3–♯5–7)
Minor 7th ♭5 chord:	Minor 3rd, diminished 5th, and minor 7th (1–♭3–♭5–♭7)
Dominant 7th ♯5 chord:	Major 3rd, augmented 5th, and minor 7th (1–3–♯5–♭7)

If we construct four-part chords from each degree of the major scale, and stay within the restrictions of the scale, we create diatonic four-part chords. The following example shows the **diatonic** four-part chords found within the C major scale:

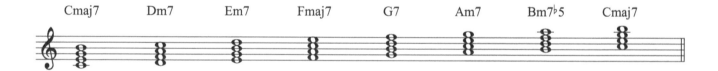

Relating the above four-part chords to those previously shown, note that major 7th chords are built from the 1st and 4th major scale degrees, minor 7th chords are built from the 2nd, 3rd, and 6th scale degrees, a dominant 7th chord is built from the 5th scale degree, and a minor 7♭5 (abbreviated as **m7♭5**) chord is built from the 7th scale degree.

major 7	minor 7	minor 7	major 7	dominant 7	minor 7	minor 7 (♭5)
Imaj7	iim7	iiim7	IVmaj7	V7	vim7	viim7♭5

Many smooth jazz progressions use these diatonic four-part chords, so you should, again, strive to learn these in as many keys as possible.

Ninth (five-part) chords and alterations

The term "ninth chord" is sometimes used to describe five-part chords in which the highest note or extension is the 9th. The five-part chords most commonly used in smooth jazz are the **major 9th**, **minor 9th**, **dominant 9th**, and **suspended dominant 9th** chords. The following example shows these four-part chords, built from the root C:

These five-part chords can all be formed by adding a **major 9th** interval to each of the four-part chords (major 7th, minor 7th, dominant 7th, suspended dominant 7th). We can analyze the intervals in each of these five-part chords as follows:

Major 9th chord: Major 3rd, perfect 5th, major 7th, and major 9th (1–3–5–7–9)
Minor 9th chord: Minor 3rd, perfect 5th, minor 7th, and major 9th (1–♭3–5–♭7–9)
Dominant 9th chord: Major 3rd, perfect 5th, minor 7th, and major 9th (1–3–5–♭7–9)
Suspended Dominant 9th chord: Perfect 4th, perfect 5th, minor 7th, and major 9th (1–4–5–♭7–9)

It is also possible to alter the 9th by flatting or sharping it by one half step. (Altering 9ths is limited to dominant chords in conventional Western music styles; we would not normally alter 9ths on major and minor chords). This altered 9th might then be combined with an altered 5th. These are the most common combinations of dominant chord alterations in smooth jazz styles:

Note that all of these chords contain major 3rd and minor 7th intervals from the root, which is the essential structure of a dominant chord. We can analyze the intervals in each of these chords as follows:

Dominant 7th ♭9:   Major 3rd, perfect 5th, minor 7th, minor 9th (1–3–5–♭7–♭9)
Dominant 7th ♯9:   Major 3rd, perfect 5th, minor 7th, augmented 9th (1–3–5–♭7–♯9)
Dominant 7th ♭9♯5:   Major 3rd, augmented 5th, minor 7th, minor 9th (1–3–♯5–♭7–♭9)
Dominant 7th ♯9♯5:   Major 3rd, augmented 5th, minor 7th, augmented 9th (1–3–♯5–♭7–♯9)

Sometimes you may encounter the suffix "7alt," as in the chord symbol C7alt. This means that all alterations of the 5th and 9th are available on the dominant chord. A good "default" response when you see a chord symbol with this suffix is to sharp the 5th and the 9th, as in the above C7♯9♯5 chord. This is a particularly useful and common sound in smooth jazz styles. In addition, you should be aware that the sharped 5th is equivalent to a flatted 13th, and the flatted 5th is equivalent to a sharped 11th. These suffixes are often used interchangeably within dominant chord symbols.

⌒

In this chapter, I've tried to summarize the essential music theory and harmony that will help you play smooth jazz on the piano. If you would like further information on these topics, please check out my other music instruction books, *Contemporary Music Theory (Levels 1–3)* and *The Pop Piano Book.* (All of these books are published by Hal Leonard Corporation.)

Chapter 3

SMOOTH JAZZ KEYBOARD HARMONY and VOICINGS

Voicing concepts

Although it is important that you know how to spell the chords described in Chapter 2, be aware that the larger the chords get (especially ninth chords and above), the less likely you are to "voice" them on the keyboard in simple ascending note stacks. A keyboard **voicing** is a specific allocation of notes between the hands, chosen to interpret the chord symbol in question. In other words, knowing how to spell the chords is one thing, but knowing how to voice them on the keyboard is quite another.

In smooth jazz styles, we will often make use of **upper-structure** voicings. These are three- or four-part interior chords that are in turn "built from" a chord tone (3rd, 5th, 7th, etc.) of the overall chord needed. Many of the triads and four-part chords we reviewed in the last chapter will also function as upper structures on larger chords. This is a very efficient voicing method, not least because the same upper structures can be used within various different overall chords.

The voicings shown in this chapter use the upper structures in the right hand played over the root of the overall chord in the left hand. This voicing concept is also used in Chapter 4 as we create rhythmic comping parts in smooth jazz styles. In Chapter 5, we'll develop melody and solo ideas in the right hand, with the left hand playing the upper-structure voicing. The root of the overall chord is provided by the bass in the rhythm section recording, which together with the piano left-hand voicing defines the overall chord. This is a common ensemble technique in smooth jazz, and indeed in jazz styles generally.

Major triad inversions

As we will shortly see, the major triad is a very commonly used upper structure on various different overall chords. Here are the inversions of a C major triad:

TRACK 1

In the above example, the first triad shown is in **root position** (with the root on the bottom), the second triad is in **first inversion** (with the 3rd on the bottom), and the third triad is in **second inversion** (with the 5th on the bottom). The last triad is in root position, an octave higher than the first. To connect smoothly between successive voicings, it is important to have these inversions under your fingers in all keys. You should make it a goal to learn all the major triad inversions, as follows:

TRACK 2

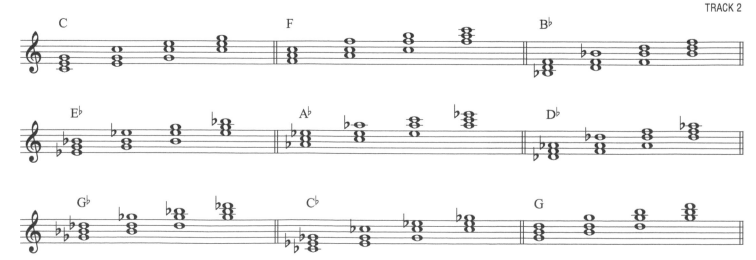

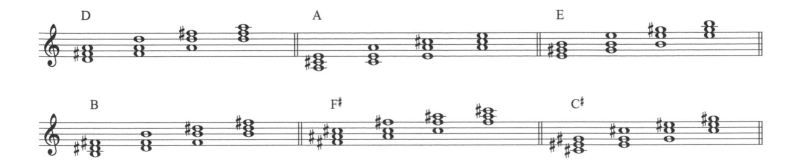

Minor triad inversions

The minor triad is also very useful as an upper-structure voicing. Here are the inversions of a C minor triad:

TRACK 3

The above example contains C minor triads in root position, first inversion, second inversion, and then root position again (similar to the previous major triad examples).

Again, you should learn these inversions in all keys, as shown in the following example:

TRACK 4

15

"Triad-over-root" chord voicings

The first upper-structure technique we will present is the "triad-over-root" voicing. Different rules will apply depending upon what overall type of chord (major, minor, dominant, etc.) we are trying to create. First we will look at the commonly used triad-over-root voicings for major chords:

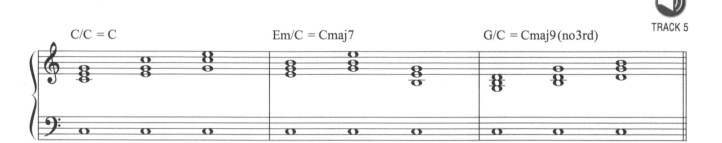

TRACK 5

We can make some observations about this example, which will apply to all the upper-structure voicings shown in this chapter.

First, one of the tones of the overall chord is the root of the upper-structure triad. In other words, the upper structures in the right hand (triads in this case) are each built from different chord tones of the overall chord (from the root, 3rd, and 5th of C major in this case). In Track 5, each inversion of the upper structure is shown in the right hand. The root of the overall chord is played by the left hand each time.

Next, there are two chord symbols above each measure. The first is a **slash chord** symbol, with the upper structure on the left of the slash, and the root note on the right. The second is the equivalent **composite** symbol, showing the overall chord created by placing the upper structure over the root.

Although both slash and composite are valid chord symbol styles, you are generally more likely to see composite symbols in a chart or fakebook. In order to use this upper-structure voicing technique, you will therefore need to be able to derive a slash chord from a composite chord symbol. There are normally two ways this is done:

- **Literal translation**: using an upper-structure voicing which when placed over the root is exactly equivalent to the composite symbol. For example, if you see the chord symbol Cmaj7 and you respond with the second voicing shown above (Em/C), you have exactly created a Cmaj7 chord between the hands with no additional notes.

- **Upgrading**: using an upper-structure voicing which when placed over the root adds more notes (extensions) to the composite symbol. For example, if you see the chord symbol Cmaj7 and you respond with the third voicing shown (G/C), you have added the 9th (and also removed the 3rd). While not appropriate in all situations, this type of upgrade can often sound very cool!

We can analyze these specific major chord voicings as follows:

- In the first measure, we are building a major triad from the root of the overall major chord: C/C. This is a simple triad-over-root voicing and just creates a basic major chord.

- In the second measure, we are building a minor triad from the 3rd of the overall major chord: Em/C. This creates a major 7th chord overall.

- In the third measure, we are building a major triad from the 5th of the overall major chord: G/C. This creates a major 9th chord (with the 3rd omitted).

Play each of these voicings and get the sounds in your ears and the shapes under your fingers! Next we will look at triad-over-root voicings for minor and suspended dominant chords:

TRACK 6

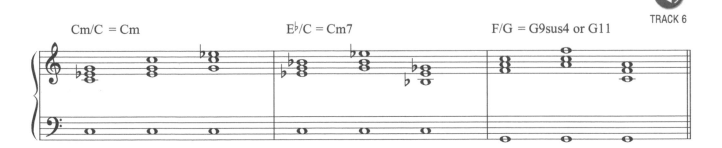

We can analyze these chord voicings as follows:

- In the first measure, we are building a minor triad from the root of the overall minor chord: Cm/C. This is a simple triad-over-root voicing and just creates a basic minor chord.

- In the second measure, we are building a major triad from the 3rd of the overall minor chord: E♭/C. This creates a minor 7th chord overall. (Note that E♭ is a minor third interval above the root of C.)

- In the third measure, we are building a major triad from the 7th of the overall suspended dominant chord: F/G. This creates a suspended dominant ninth (a.k.a. dominant eleventh) chord. (Note that F is a minor 7th interval above the root G.) The term suspended means that the 3rd of the dominant chord (B) has been replaced by the 4th/11th (C). This voicing can also work as a less defined or "incomplete minor" 11th chord.

Again, there are voicing upgrade possibilities here. For example, it is common practice in many contemporary styles (including smooth jazz) to upgrade basic minor triad chord symbols by building the major triad from the 3rd, creating a minor 7th chord overall.

Next we will look at triad-over-root voicings for altered minor 7th and dominant 7th chords:

TRACK 7

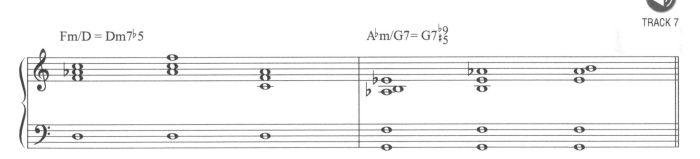

We can analyze these chord voicings as follows:

- In the first measure, we are building a minor triad from the 3rd of the overall minor chord: Fm/D. This creates a minor 7th with flatted 5th chord overall. (Note that F is a minor 3rd interval above the root of D.)

- In the second measure, we are building a minor triad from the flatted 9th of the overall dominant chord (A♭m/G7, with the 7th added above the root in the left hand). This creates a dominant 7th with sharped 5th and flatted 9th chord overall. The root–7th interval in the left hand helps define the dominant chord and is commonly used in jazz styles. (Note that A♭ is a minor 9th interval above the root G, also equivalent to an octave plus a half step.)

Now we'll see how to move between chords using these voicings and inversions. We'll start with a I–ii–V (chords built from the 1st, 2nd, and 5th degrees of the key) progression in C major:

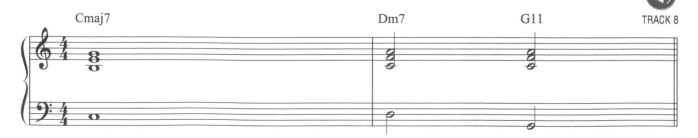

TRACK 8

Note that we no longer have the triad-over-root (or "slash") chord symbols above the staff—just the composite symbols (a realistic situation when we are interpreting a chart or fake book). We need to look at each of these symbols and derive a triad-over-root voicing for each one. Then we need to **voice lead** smoothly between these upper-structure triads by using inversions to avoid unnecessary interval skips. We can summarize the voicing choices as follows:

- In the first measure, the Cmaj7 chord is voiced by building a minor triad from the 3rd: Em/C.

- In the second measure (beat 1), the Dm7 chord is voiced by building a major triad from the 3rd: F/D.

- In the second measure (beat 3), the G11 chord is voiced by building a major triad from the 7th: F/G.

All the upper-structure triads were in second inversion, resulting in smooth voice leading through the progression. Now we will apply a simple eighth-note rhythm pattern to these voicings:

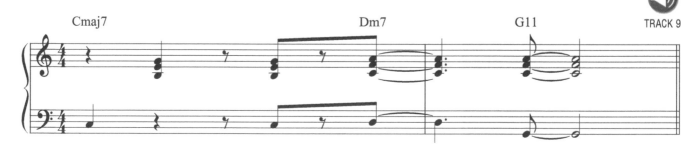

TRACK 9

This type of two-measure progression is often repeated (creating a **vamp**) in smooth jazz styles to accompany a melody or solo. Next we'll create voicings for another I–ii–V progression, this time in the key of C minor:

TRACK 10

Notice that we now have the key signature for C minor (three flats) at the beginning of each staff. Again, we have interpreted the composite chord symbols with triad-over-root voicings, as follows:

- In the first measure, the Cm7 chord is voiced by building a major triad from the 3rd: E♭/C.

- In the second measure (beat 1), the Dm7♭5 chord is voiced by building a minor triad from the 3rd: Fm/D.

- In the second measure (beat 3), the G7♭9♯5 chord is voiced by building a minor triad from the ♭9th in the right hand, over a root–7th interval in the left hand: A♭m/G7.

We can apply the same rhythmic pattern to these voicings, as follows:

TRACK 11

Major seventh chord inversions

The major 7th four-part chord is another useful upper structure on some larger chords. Here are the close-voiced inversions of a C major 7th chord:

TRACK 12

The first chord shown is in **root position** (with the root on the bottom), the second chord is in **first inversion** (with the 3rd on the bottom), the third chord is in **second inversion** (with the 5th on the bottom), and the fourth chord is in **third inversion** (with the 7th on the bottom). Note that the first inversion major 7th chord sounds more dissonant due to the "exposed" half-step interval on top, and this inversion should therefore be used with some care. You should make it a goal to learn all the major 7th chord inversions, as follows:

TRACK 13

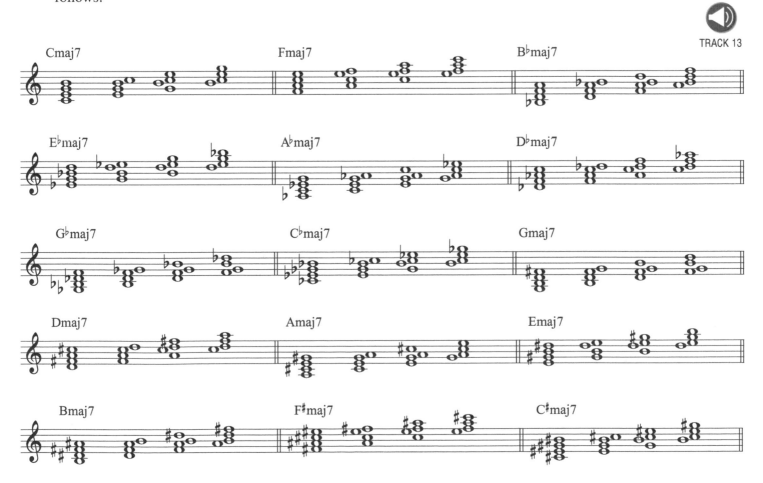

19

Minor seventh chord inversions

The minor 7th four-part chord, like the major 7th, is also a useful upper structure on larger chords. Here are the inversions of a C minor 7th chord:

TRACK 14

The above example contains C minor 7th chords in root position, first inversion, second inversion, and third inversion (similar to the previous major 7th chord examples).

Again, you should learn these inversions in all keys, as shown in the following example:

TRACK 15

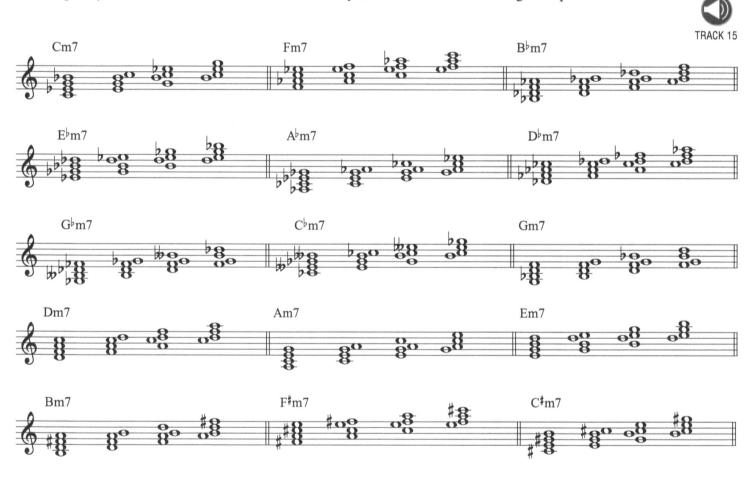

We saw in Chapter 2 that a minor 7th chord can be altered to a minor 7♭5 chord by flatting the 5th. The minor 7♭5 chord is a useful upper structure when voicing dominant and altered harmonies. Here are the first three minor 7♭5 chords and inversions around the circle of 5ths, and it is again recommended that you become familiar with these in all keys:

TRACK 16

"Four-part-over-root" chord voicings

The next upper-structure technique we will look at is the "four-part-over-root" voicing. This involves building a four-part interior chord from a chord tone (3rd, 5th, 7th, etc.) of the overall chord. Again, different rules will apply depending upon what type of chord (major, minor, dominant, etc.) we are trying to create. First we will look at the commonly used four-part-over-root voicings for major and minor chords:

TRACK 17

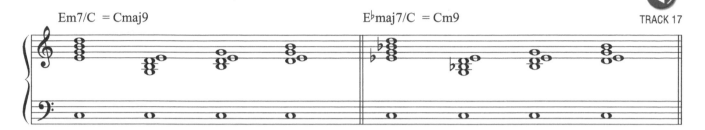

As for the triad-over-root voicings, both slash chord and composite chord symbols are shown, and all inversions of the upper structures are shown. Again, the goal is to be able to interpret the composite symbol with a suitable upper-structure voicing. We can analyze the above voicings as follows:

- In the first measure, we are building a minor 7th four-part chord from the 3rd of the overall major chord: Em7/C. This creates a major 9th chord overall.

- In the second measure, we are building a major 7th four-part chord from the 3rd of the overall minor chord: E♭maj7/C. (E♭ is a minor 3rd interval above the root of C). This creates a minor 9th chord overall.

It is common practice in smooth jazz styles (as well as in pop/R&B) to upgrade major 7th chord symbols by using the first voicing above, and to upgrade minor 7th chord symbols by using the second voicing above. In both cases the net result is to add the 9th of the chord. In some cases we might even upgrade basic major and minor triad symbols this way (which would then add the 7th and 9th) to provide more density and sophistication, if needed.

Next we will look at a series of four-part-over-root voicings for dominant and suspended dominant chords:

TRACK 18

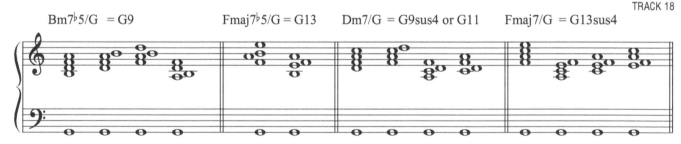

Note that the first two measures above contain voicings for regular, non-suspended dominant chords, which all contain the 3rd (B) and 7th (F) of the overall chord. The last two measures contain voicings for suspended dominant chords, in which the 3rd (B) has been replaced by the 4th/11th (C). These suspended voicings still contain the 7th of the chord (F). The above voicings are further analyzed as follows:

- In the first measure, we are building a m7♭5 four-part chord from the 3rd of the overall dominant chord, Bm7♭5/G. This creates a dominant 9th chord overall.

- In the second measure, we are building a maj7♭5 four-part chord from the 7th of the overall dominant chord, Fmaj7♭5/G. This creates a dominant 13th chord overall.

- In the third measure, we are building a minor 7th four-part chord from the 5th of the overall suspended dominant chord, Dm7/G. This creates a suspended dominant 9th (or dominant 11th) chord overall.

- In the fourth measure, we are building a major 7th four-part chord from the 7th of the overall suspended dominant chord, Fmaj7/G. This creates a suspended dominant 13th chord overall.

When building upper structures from the 7th of the chord in measures 2 and 4 of the last example, don't forget that F is a minor 7th interval above the root of G. Also, note that in the second measure, the Fmaj7♭5 upper structure is only shown in root position and second inversion, as these are the most useful for this particular voicing. Next we have some four-part-over-root voicings for altered dominant chords:

TRACK 19

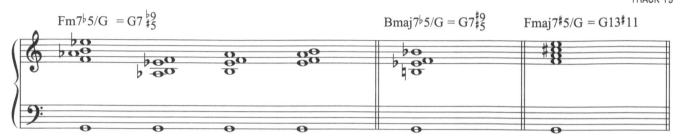

When notating these voicings, decisions are sometimes needed between different enharmonic alternatives (i.e., A♯ or B♭) for the same note. Generally it is recommended to notate in a manner consistent with the key or scale being used. The above altered G7 voicings will most often function as V chords in the key of C minor, so the top note in the second measure (the sharped 9th on the G7) has been notated as B♭ rather than A♯ for consistency with the implied key. These voicings are further analyzed as follows:

- In the first measure, we are building a m7♭5 four-part chord from the 7th of the overall dominant chord, Fm7♭5/G. This creates a dominant 7th with flatted 9th and sharped 5th chord overall.

- In the second measure, we are building a maj7♭5 four-part chord from the 3rd of the overall dominant chord, Bmaj7♭5/G. This creates a dominant 7th with sharped 9th and sharped 5th chord overall.

- In the third measure, we are building a maj7♯5 four-part chord from the 7th of the overall dominant chord, Fmaj7♯5/G. This creates a dominant 13th with sharped 11th chord overall. (Remember from Chapter 2 that a sharped 11th is equivalent to a flatted 5th on the chord).

As in the previous dominant voicings, when building upper structures from the 7th of the chord, note that the starting note of the upper structure is a minor seventh interval above the root of the overall chord. Some upper structures are shown in root position only, as this often works best on these more complex altered dominant chords.

Now we'll see how to move between chords using these four-part-over-root voicings and inversions. We'll start with a I–IV–V progression in C major (chords built from the 1st, 4th, and 5th degrees of the key):

TRACK 20

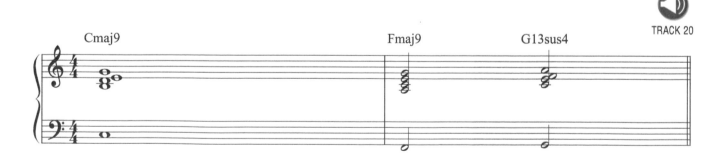

Again, we are just showing the composite chord symbols, and our job is to interpret these with suitable upper-structure voicings. As with the previous triad-over-root progressions, once we have selected the four-part upper structures, we then need to invert them to ensure smooth voice leading.

- In the first measure, the Cmaj9 chord is voiced by building a minor 7th four-part chord from the 3rd: Em7/C.

- In the second measure (beat 1), the Fmaj9 chord is also voiced by building a minor 7th four-part chord from the 3rd: Am7/F.

- In the second measure (beat 3), the G13sus4 chord is voiced by building a major 7th four-part chord from the 7th: Fmaj7/G.

Now we can apply a smooth jazz rhythmic comping pattern to these voicings:

TRACK 21

This pattern uses a sixteenth-note anticipation of beat 4, which is a common smooth jazz figure. (In Chapter 4, we'll explore many more comping patterns and rhythms.) Next, we'll create four-part-over-root voicings for another I–IV–V progression, this time in the key of C minor:

TRACK 22

We now have the key signature for C minor, three flats, at the beginning of each staff. This time the composite chord symbols have been voiced as follows:

- In the first measure, the Cm9 chord is voiced by building a major 7th four-part chord from the 3rd: E♭maj7/C.

- In the second measure (beat 1), the Fm9 chord is also voiced by building a major 7th four-part chord from the 3rd: A♭maj7/F.

- In the second measure (beat 3), the G7#9#5 chord is voiced by building a major 7th♭5 four-part chord from the 3rd: Bmaj7♭5/G.

Note that the upper structures on the minor chords are built from minor 3rd intervals, but the upper structure on the dominant chord is built from the major 3rd interval. We can apply the same rhythmic pattern to these voicings, as follows:

TRACK 23

"Seven-three" extended chord voicings

We will now develop the "seven-three" extended voicing technique for dominant chords. This involves playing the 7th and 3rd of the chord (which are the definitive "character" tones) plus one alteration, creating a three-note shape in total. Like the other voicings so far in this chapter, "7-3" extended voicings are used in the right hand for smooth jazz comping and also in the left hand to support a melody or solo. Here are the most commonly used 7-3 extended voicings for dominant chords in smooth jazz styles:

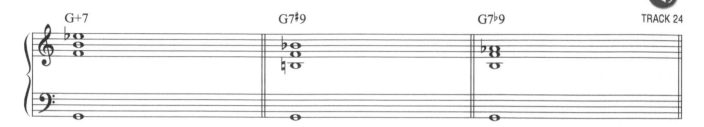

All of these voicings use the 7th and 3rd of the dominant chord in the right hand, over the root in the left hand. Then the sharped 5th is added above the 3rd in the first measure, and the sharped 9th and flatted 9th are added above the 7th in the second and third measures, respectively. (These alterations are again enharmonically notated for consistency with the implied key of C minor.) Now we will combine two voicing techniques ("7-3 extended" and "four-part-over-root") to create voicings for a I–♭VI–II–V progression in C minor:

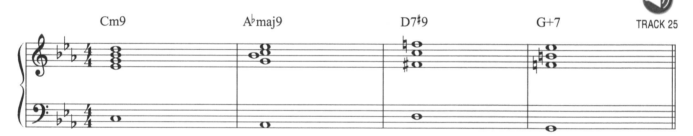

Here is a summary of these voicing choices:

*   In the first measure, the Cm9 chord is voiced by building a major 7th four-part chord from the 3rd: E♭maj7/C.

*   In the second measure, the A♭maj9 chord is voiced by building a minor 7th four-part chord from the 3rd: Cm7/A♭.

*   In the third measure, the D7♯9 chord is voiced using the 7-3 extended technique, adding the ♯9th (F) above the 7th.

*   In the fourth measure, the G+7 chord is also voiced using 7-3 extended, adding the ♯5th (E♭) above the 3rd.

Now we'll apply another smooth jazz rhythmic comping pattern to these voicings:

Rhythmically speaking, the right-hand part is anticipating beat 2 by a sixteenth note and beat 3 by an eighth note in each measure. The left hand is repeating the root of the chord on beat 4 of each measure.

"Double 4th" shapes and chord voicings

Our final voicing technique in this chapter uses what I call "double 4th" shapes. These are three-note voicings creating by stacking two perfect fourth intervals on top of one another. I use the term "shape" when referring to these, as they are not easily or helpfully described with individual chord symbols, unlike the triad and four-part voicings earlier in this chapter. Their interchangeability within different overall chords makes double 4th shapes excellent choices for upper-structure voicings. First let's look at the double 4th shape, together with some inversions and octave doubling variations:

TRACK 27

In the first measure, we begin with a root-position double 4th (D–G–C). After this, the shape is then shown in first and second inversions. In the second measure, we start by combining the first and second inversions together (doubling the G an octave below), and then we combine the second inversion and root position (doubling the C an octave below). These are all useful variations and signature sounds in contemporary jazz styles. Now we'll see how to use this shape to create "double-4th-over-root" voicings for major, minor, and dominant chords:

TRACK 28

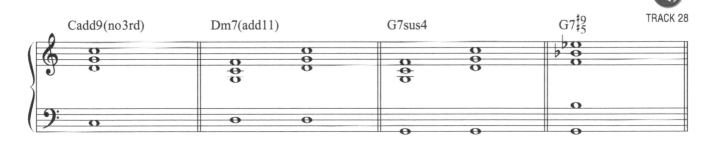

We can analyze the above voicings as follows:

- In the first measure, we are building a double 4th (D–G–C) from the 9th of the overall major chord. This creates a major chord with added 9th and 3rd omitted overall.

- In the second measure, we are building a double 4th (G–C–F) from the 4th/11th, and a double 4th (D–G–C) from the root of the overall minor chord. These voicings create a minor 7th chord with added 4th/11th overall.

- In the third measure, we are building a double 4th (G–C–F) from the root and a double 4th (D–G–C) from the 5th of the overall suspended dominant chord. These create a suspended dominant 7th chord overall.

- In the fourth measure, we are building a double 4th (F–B♭–E♭) from the 7th of the overall altered dominant chord. Together with the 3rd added in the left hand, this creates a dominant 7th with sharped 9th and sharped 5th chord overall. (Don't worry if you can't stretch enough to play the left-hand interval—just transpose the bottom G up an octave.)

Although we have used detailed chord symbols in the previous example (to describe the extensions or alterations added with the double 4ths), in practice the smooth jazz keyboardist will often use these voicings to upgrade basic major, minor, or dominant chord symbols on a chart. Also note that the inversions and octave doubling shown in Track 27 can be applied to all of the double-4th-over-root voicings above.

Next, we will create double-4th-over-root voicings to upgrade a basic I–ii–iii–V progression in D major:

TRACK 29

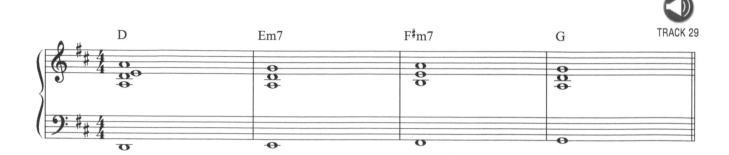

We can analyze these voicings as follows:

- In the first measure, we are building a double 4th (E–A–D) from the 9th of the D major chord. The right hand is combining the first and second inversions of the shape, doubling the top note A an octave below. This adds a 9th to (and removes the 3rd from) the chord.

- In the second measure, we are building a double 4th (A–D–G) from the 4th/11th of the E minor 7th chord. This adds the 4th/11th to the chord.

- In the third measure, we are building a double 4th (B–E–A) from the 4th/11th of the F♯ minor 7th chord. This adds the 4th/11th to the chord.

- In the fourth measure, we are building a double 4th (A–D–G) from the 9th of the G major chord. This adds a 9th to (and removes the 3rd from) the chord.

Let's use these new voicings in a rhythmic comping example:

TRACK 30

Listen to the sophisticated, yet clean and transparent sound that is produced when using double-4th-over-root voicings to upgrade basic chord symbols. This technique is very useful in more evolved rock and R&B, as well as in contemporary jazz styles.

Chapter 4

SMOOTH JAZZ
PROGRESSIONS and COMPING

Now we get to apply the keyboard harmony covered in Chapter 3 to create authentic **comping** (accompaniment) patterns in a wide variety of smooth jazz styles. We'll begin by reviewing the rhythmic subdivisions used in smooth jazz.

Rhythmic concepts

Almost all smooth jazz comping uses patterns based around eighth notes or sixteenth notes. Each of these subdivisions can be played **straight** or with a **swing** feel, essentially resulting in four main rhythmic styles or groups:

- Straight eighths
- Swing eighths
- Straight sixteenths
- Swing sixteenths

Every example in this book from now on will fall into one of these rhythmic categories. In straight eighths, each eighth note is of equal length and divides the beat exactly in half, as follows:

TRACK 31

Notice the rhythmic counting above the staff. This is how eighth-note rhythms are normally counted, with the 1, 2, 3, and 4 falling on the **downbeats**, and the "ands" falling halfway in between on the **upbeats**.

In a swing eighths feel, the second eighth note in each beat (the "and" in the rhythmic counting) lands two-thirds of the way through the beat. This is equivalent to playing on the first and third parts of an eighth-note triplet. We still count using "1 and 2 and" etc., but now each "and" is played a little later:

TRACK 32

The first measure above looks the same as the previous straight eighths example, but when a swing eighths interpretation is applied to it, it sounds equivalent to the second measure above (quarter-eighth triplets). As the second measure above is more cumbersome to write and to read, it is common practice to notate as in the first measure above, but to rhythmically interpret in a swing eighths style as needed.

There will also be times when we need to access the middle note (the second of three notes) in an eighth-note triplet within an overall swing eighths feel. In this case we would notate using a triplet sign, but all the other eighth-note pairs (without triplet signs) would still be interpreted as swing eighths. If a tune needs a lot of triplet signs for this reason, we should consider notating in 12/8 time as an alternative to 4/4, which would expose all of the eighth notes without a need for triplet signs.

In a sixteenth-note feel, all the "ands" or eighth-note upbeats will fall exactly halfway between the down-beats. However, each eighth note will now be subdivided differently when comparing straight sixteenth and swing sixteenths rhythmic feels. In a straight sixteenth feel, each sixteenth note is of equal length and divides the eighth note exactly in half (and the beat exactly into quarters) as follows:

TRACK 33

Again note the rhythmic counting above the staff—this is how sixteenth-note rhythms are normally counted. In between the beat numbers (1, 2, 3, 4) and the "ands", we have the "e" on the 2nd sixteenth note and the "a" on the 4th sixteenth note within each beat.

In a swing sixteenths feel, the 2nd and 4th sixteenth notes in each beat (the "e" and "a" in the rhythmic counting) land two-thirds of the way through each eighth note, rather than dividing it in half. This is equiv-alent to playing on the first and third parts of a sixteenth-note triplet. We still count using "1 e and a" etc., but now each "e" and "a" is played a little later:

TRACK 34

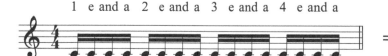 

Note that the first measure above looks the same as the previous straight sixteenths example, but when a swing sixteenths interpretation is applied to it, its sound is equivalent to the second measure above: the eighth-sixteenth triplets.

Now we will look at various smooth jazz comping grooves and progressions for the piano, and we'll see that the **form**, or structure, of smooth jazz tunes is normally built around two-, four-, or eight-measure sections. In Chapter 6 we'll see how these sections are combined to create complete tunes in smooth jazz styles.

The play-along audio contains two tracks for each of the comping examples in this chapter. The first track is piano only, with the left-hand part on the left channel, the right-hand part on the right channel and the high hat quarter-note click in the middle. This enables you to practice each hand separately by turning down one channel or the other. The second track has a smooth jazz rhythm section on the left channel and the piano part (left and right hands) on the right channel. To play along with the band on these examples, turn down the right channel. All these comping examples use upper-structure voicings in the right hand and single-note patterns in the left hand.

We'll start with a straight eighths pattern in the style of "Stevie Wonderful" by the noted smooth jazz pianist Gregg Karukas. This uses a Rhodes-style electric piano sound with chorus applied, a favorite smooth jazz keyboard sound. Note that the left and right hands are collectively arpeggiating each chord on the "1 and 2 and" of each measure and anticipating beat 3. The left hand plays the root and 5th of each chord, while the right hand uses triad-over-root voicings, rhythmically "split" or arpeggiated.

Straight eighths groove #1 – Style of "Stevie Wonderful"

TRACK 35
piano only

TRACK 36
piano plus
rhythm section

This example uses a i–ii–♭VI–iv progression in the key of B♭ minor. The right-hand voicings used are as follows:

*   In measure 1, B♭m7 is voiced by building a major triad from the 3rd: D♭/B♭.

*   In measure 2, Cm7 is voiced by building a major triad from the 3rd: E♭/C.

*   In measure 3, the chord symbol prompts us to build a major triad from the 5th: D♭/G♭, creating a major 9th (with the 3rd omitted) chord overall.

*   In measure 4, E♭m7 is voiced by building a major triad from the 3rd: G♭/E♭.

The same voicings are repeated for measures 5–8. The eighth-note fills in the right hand at the end of the even-numbered measures are either arpeggiated notes from the upper-structure triad or notes from the B♭ minor scale that are available within the right-hand position.

Our next straight eighths comping pattern is in the style of "She Likes to Watch" by the Rippingtons. This has an uptempo feel with more eighth-note anticipations. This groove uses a Yamaha DX-style electric piano, a popular sound since the mid-1980s. The left and right hands are playing the voicings simultaneously, in the same rhythm, interspersed with octave riffs in both hands, as follows:

Straight eighths groove #2 – Style of "She Likes to Watch"

TRACK 37
piano only

TRACK 38
piano plus
rhythm section

Straight Eighths Groove #2 is in the key of D minor, and the octave riffs in measures 4 and 12 come from the D minor pentatonic scale. The rhythm section uses a synth bass and drum machine samples for an electronic feel, adding a string synth along with the electric piano part. In the last eight measures, an acoustic piano melody is introduced that is supported by the comping pattern. The right-hand voicings used in measures 9–16 are the same as for measures 1–8, which we can analyze as follows:

- In measures 1, 3, and 5, Dm7 is voiced by building a major triad from the 3rd: F/D.

- In measures 1, 2, 3, and 5, Am7 is voiced by building a major triad from the 3rd: C/A, with octave doubling within the upper triad in measure 2.

- In measure 1, B♭maj7 is voiced by building a minor triad from the 3rd: Dm/B♭.

- In measure 3, Gm7 is voiced by building a major triad from the 3rd: B♭/G.

- In measure 4, C11 is voiced by building a minor 7th four-part chord from the 5th: Gm7/C.

- In measure 6, C/F symbol prompts us to build a major triad from the 5th, creating a major 9th (with the 3rd omitted) chord overall.

- In measure 6, B♭maj9 is voiced by building a minor 7th four-part chord from the 3rd: Dm7/B♭.

- In measure 8, C13sus4 is voiced by building a major 7th four-part chord from the 7th: B♭maj7/C.

Next we will look at a swing eighths groove in the style of "I Meant What I Said" by Gregg Karukas. As noted earlier in this chapter, we sometimes need to notate eighth-note triplets in a swing eighths feel, whenever we need to access the middle note within the triplet. Otherwise, all eighth-note pairs without triplet signs will be interpreted as swing eighths.

Swing eighths groove #1 – Style of "I Meant What I Said"

TRACK 39
piano only

TRACK 40
piano plus
rhythm section

31

Swing Eighths Groove #1 starts in the key of E minor and transitions into its relative major, G, in measure 9. The pattern uses an acoustic piano sound, and a synth pad is added to the piano comping towards the end. Here are the right-hand voicings used:

- In measures 1 and 5, Em7 is voiced by building a major triad from the 3rd: G/E.

- In measures 1, 3, 5, and 7, Am7 is voiced by building a major triad from the 3rd: C/A.

- In measures 2 and 6, F#7#9 is voiced using the 7-3 extended voicing technique (3–7–#9 from bottom to top).

- In measures 2 and 6, B+7 is voiced using 7-3 extended (7–3–#5 from bottom to top).

- In measures 3 and 7, the G/C chord symbol prompts us to build a major triad from the 5th, creating a major 9th (with the 3rd omitted) chord overall.

- In measures 4 and 8, D11 is voiced by building a minor 7th four-part chord from the 5th: Am7/D, and by building a major triad from the 7th: C/D.

- In measures 9 and 13, Gmaj7 is voiced by building a minor triad from the 3rd: Bm/G.

- In measures 10 and 12, the Am7/G chord symbol prompts us to invert Am7 over its 7th (G). This functions as a "passing chord" between the Gmaj7 and Gmaj9 chords.

- In measure 11, Gmaj9 is voiced by building a minor 7th four-part chord from the 3rd: Bm7/G.

This groove has a busier and more "linear" left-hand part than the previous examples. Various root-7th, root-5th, and octave intervals are used, and the eighth-note triplets inside beat 2 connect effectively into the chord changes anticipating beat 3. The right-hand embellishments are partial or arpeggiated upper structures with some scalar passing tones.

Let's move on to some patterns using sixteenth-note subdivisions. The next example is a straight sixteenths groove in the style of "Chopsticks" by Jeff Lorber. This uses a Rhodes-style electric piano sound and consists of two eight-measure sections. The first eight measures have both hands playing sustained voicings simultaneously, anticipating beat 2 of each measure by an eighth note. The next eight measures use the same voicings in a funkier sixteenth-note comping rhythm.

Straight sixteenths groove #1 – Style of "Chopsticks"

TRACK 41
piano only

TRACK 42
piano plus
rhythm section

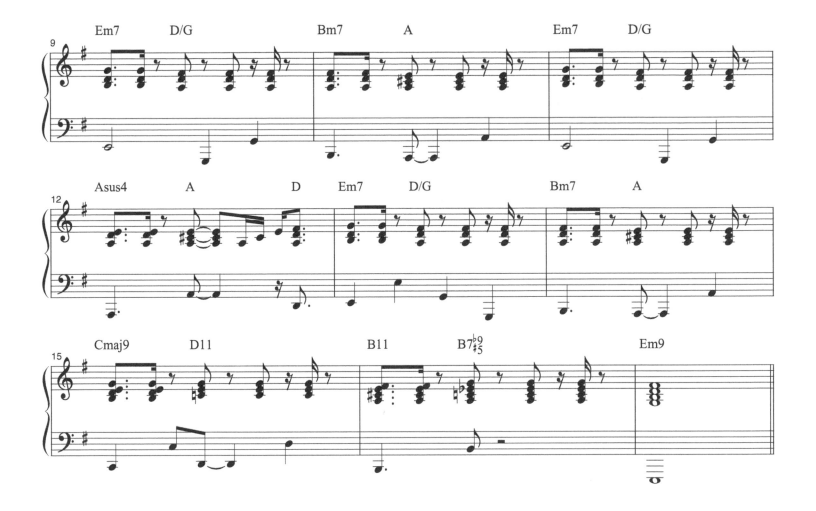

This progression is in the key of E minor. Note the funky sixteenth-note subdivisions beginning in measure 9, with the right-hand upper structure landing on the last sixteenth of beat 1, and the 2nd sixteenth of beat 4. On the rhythm section track, a synth clav part is added to spice up the groove at this point. The right-hand voicings used in measures 9–16 are the same as for measures 1–8.

- In measures 1, 3, and 5, Em7 is voiced by building a major triad from the 3rd: G/E.

- In measures 1, 3, and 5, D/G symbol prompts us to build a major triad from the 5th, creating a major 9th (with the 3rd omitted) chord overall.

- In measures 2 and 6, Bm7 is voiced by building a major triad from the 3rd: D/B.

- In measures 2, 4, and 6, A is voiced simply by building a major triad from the root: A/A.

- In measure 4, the Asus4 chord is voiced by suspending the A triad: replacing the 3rd (C#) with the 4th (D).

- In measure 4, the D chord is voiced simply by building a major triad from the root: D/D.

- In measure 7, Cmaj9 is voiced by building a minor 7th four-part chord from the 3rd: Em7/C.

- In measure 7, D11 is voiced by building a major triad from the 7th: C/D.

- In measure 8, B11 is voiced by building a minor 7th four-part chord from the 5th: F#m7/B.

- In measure 8, B7♭9#5 is voiced by building a m7♭5 four-part chord from the 7th: Am7♭5/B.

- In measure 17, Em9 is voiced by building a major 7th four-part chord from the 3rd: Gmaj7/E.

Next up is another straight sixteenths groove in the style of "Baby Come to Me" by George Howard. This has a mellower feel, with the right hand using eighth-note anticipations and sixteenth-note arpeggios as fills. A Yamaha DX-style electric piano is used on the track.

Straight sixteenths groove #2 — Style of "Baby Come to Me"

TRACK 43
piano only

TRACK 44
piano plus
rhythm section

This progression is in the key of C minor. The left hand is often playing "pickups" an eighth note ahead of the right hand. For instance, in measure 5 the left-hand E♭ lands on beat 2, an eighth note ahead of the right-hand voicing on the "and" of 2, and again on the "and" of 3, an eighth note ahead of the right-hand arpeggio starting on beat 4. This all helps to impart forward motion to the arrangement. The rhythm section track adds a marimba-type pattern and sparse acoustic piano fills to complement the piano comping. The arpeggios and embellishments in the right-hand part are based upon the upper-structure voicings, which are derived as follows:

- In measures 1 and 9, Cm7 is voiced by building a major triad from the 3rd: E♭/C.

- In measures 2 and 10, Fm9 is voiced by building a major 7th four-part chord from the 3rd: A♭maj7/F.

- In measures 3 and 11, Dm7♭5 is voiced by building a minor triad from the 3rd: Fm/D.

- In measures 4, 8, and 12, the Gsus4 chord is voiced by suspending the G triad: replacing the 3rd (B) with the 4th (C).

- In measures 4, 8, and 12, the G+7 chord is voiced using 7-3 extended (7–3–♯5 from bottom to top), with the left hand playing the 7th and the right hand playing the 3rd and ♯5th.

- In measure 5, A♭maj9 is voiced by building a minor 7th four-part chord from the 3rd: Cm7/A♭.

- In measure 6, Fm7 is voiced by building a major triad from the 3rd: A♭/F, with octave doubling.

- In measure 7, D♭maj9 is voiced by building a minor 7th four-part chord from the 3rd: Fm7/D♭.
- In measure 13, Cm9 is voiced by building a major 7th four-part chord from the 3rd: E♭maj7/C.

Our next straight sixteenths groove is in the style of "Room to Breathe" by Najee and mixes some upper triad, four-part, and 7-3 extended voicing techniques. The right hand anticipates beat 3 by an eighth note, and then from measure 5 starts to add some funky sixteenth-note subdivisions—mainly on the 2nd sixteenth of beat 4. The left hand uses more pickups, often landing an eighth note or sixteenth note ahead of the right hand.

Straight sixteenths groove #3 – Style of "Room to Breathe"

TRACK 45
piano only

TRACK 46
piano plus
rhythm section

This progression is in the key of B minor, and a Rhodes-style electric piano has again been used. On the rhythm track a synth melody has been added that is supported by the piano comping. Here are the voicings and how they are obtained:

- In measure 1, Bm7 is voiced by building a major triad from the 3rd: D/B.
- In measures 2 and 6, the D11 chord is voiced by building a major triad from the 7th: C/D, with octave doubling in measure 6.
- In measures 3 and 7, Gmaj9 is voiced by building a minor 7th four-part chord from the 3rd: Bm7/G.
- In measure 4, the C♯7♯9 chord is voiced using 7-3 extended (3–7–♯9 from bottom to top).
- In measure 4, the F♯+7 chord is voiced using 7-3 extended (7–3–♯5 from bottom to top).
- In measure 8, the C♯7♯9 chord is voiced using a double 4th (7–♯9–♯5 from bottom to top), with the 3rd added in the left hand on beat 2. This upgrades the chord symbol by adding the ♯5th.
- In measure 8, the F♯7♯9 chord is voiced using 7-3 extended (3–7–♯9 from bottom to top).
- In measure 9, Bm9 is voiced by building a major 7th four-part chord from the 3rd: Dmaj7/B.

Our next groove is in the style of "Just to Be Loved" by Al Jarreau, which has a straight sixteenths ballad feel. The four-measure introduction uses some upper-structure triad voicings and arpeggios, and then from measure 5 the main groove features four-part upper structures, left-hand pickups (leading into the right hand), and anticipations of beat 4 by a sixteenth note. These piano devices work across a range of sixteenth-note ballad styles, from R&B/pop to smooth jazz.

Straight sixteenths groove #4 (ballad) — Style of "Just to Be Loved"

TRACK 47
piano only

TRACK 48
piano plus
rhythm section

This progression starts in the key of C minor and transitions into its relative major, E♭, in measure 5. The pattern was recorded using a synthesized electric piano sound. Again the left hand plays the root of each chord, and then adds the 5th, 7th, or octave afterwards as a rhythmic pickup leading into the right-hand voicing. On the rhythm section track starting in measure 5, an organ pad fills out the sound behind the piano comping, and a sparse acoustic guitar melody is added. Here is the voicing analysis:

- In measures 1 and 3, Cm7 is voiced by building a major triad from the 3rd: E♭/C, with octave doubling in measure 1.

- In measures 2 and 4, G11 is voiced by building a major triad from the 7th: F/G, with octave doubling in measure 2.

- In measure 4, A♭maj9 is voiced by building a minor 7th four-part chord from the 3rd: Cm7/A♭.

- In measures 4, 5, 7, and 9, B♭11 is voiced by building a minor 7th four-part chord from the 5th: Fm7/B♭.

- In measures 5, 7, and 9–11, E♭maj9 is voiced by building a minor 7th four-part chord from the 3rd: Gm7/E♭.

- In measures 6, 8, and 10, C♭maj9 (equivalent to Bmaj9) is voiced by building a minor 7th four-part chord from the 3rd: E♭m7/C♭.

- In measures 6, 8, and 10, A♭m7 is either voiced by building a major triad from the 3rd: C♭/A♭ with octave doubling, or by building a major 7th four-part chord from the 3rd: C♭maj7/A♭, which upgrades the chord by adding the 9th (B♭).

Finally in this chapter we will look at some swing sixteenths comping patterns. These will often borrow elements from R&B/funk and hip-hop styles, orchestrated and produced in a manner appropriate for the smooth jazz market. Our first swing sixteenths example is in the style of "Get It On" by Brian Culbertson, who is noted for his modern electronic smooth jazz recordings. This uses a **i–ii–V** repeated progression (or "vamp") in F minor similar to the Chapter 3 progression examples, voiced using four-part-over-root upper structures. In the intro (first 4 measures), the left and right hands play simultaneously, emphasizing the sixteenth-note anticipations of beats 2 and 4. Starting in measure 5, we add more sixteenth subdivisions and left-hand pickups, and then starting in measure 9, we add some 4th intervals from the A♭ pentatonic scale to create a busier groove.

Swing sixteenths groove #1 – Style of "Get It On"

TRACK 49
piano only

TRACK 50
piano plus
rhythm section

On the rhythm track of Swing Sixteenths Groove #1, a synth flute melody rides over the piano comping, and starting in measure 9 a synth pad is added to fatten up the groove. Here are the piano voicings used:

- In measures 1, 3, 5, and 7, Fm9 is voiced by building a major 7th four-part chord from the 3rd: A♭maj7/F.

- In measures 2 and 6, Gm9 is voiced by building a major 7th four-part chord from the 3rd: B♭maj7/G.

- In measures 2 and 6, C7♭9♯5 is voiced by building a m7♭5 four-part chord from the 7th: B♭m7♭5/C.

- In measures 4 and 8, D♭maj9 is voiced by building a minor 7th four-part chord from the 3rd: Fm7/D♭.

- In measures 4 and 8, E♭11 is voiced by building a minor 7th four-part chord from the 5th: B♭m7/E♭.

- In measures 9, 11, and 13, A♭maj9 is voiced by building a minor 7th four-part chord from the 3rd: Cm7/A♭, adding some 4th intervals from the A♭ pentatonic scale.

- In measures 10, 12, and 14, E♭11 is voiced by building a major triad from the 7th: D♭/E♭, with octave doubling.

- In measure 15, Fmaj9 is voiced by building a minor 7th four-part chord from the 3rd: Am7/F.

Our next swing sixteenth pattern is in the style of "Rejoyce" by David Benoit, a pianist noted for using pop and hip-hop elements in his smooth jazz stylings. This was recorded using an acoustic piano sound, Benoit's instrument of choice. This example uses double-4th-over-root voicings and two-note interval patterns in the right hand, except in measures 9–10 and 13–14, which feature triad-over-root voicings and arpeggios. The left hand is also using sixteenth-note pickups.

Swing sixteenths groove #2 — Style of "Rejoyce"

TRACK 51
piano only

TRACK 52
piano plus
rhythm section

This tune is in the key of A minor. As discussed in Chapter 3, basic major and minor chord symbols are upgraded (extensions are added) when double-4th-over-root voicings are applied. Following each double-4th shape is a series of two-note intervals in the right hand. The top note is the same note as the highest note in the double 4th (G) and is repeated over a moving line derived from the A natural minor scale. This type of repeating top note is sometimes referred to as a **drone**. The embellishments over the Dm7 and Em7 chords are all derived from the upper-structure triads used. On the rhythm track, a slow-moving synth melody is added, and the right-hand interval pattern is doubled with a marimba-type sound. The voicings used are as follows:

- In measures 1–2, 7–8, 11–12, and 15, Am7 is voiced using a double 4th (A–D–G) built from the root.

- In measures 3 and 4, F is voiced using a double 4th (A–D–G) built from the 3rd (an alternative to building this shape from the 9th on major chords). This adds the 6th and 9th to the chord.

- In measures 5–6, G is voiced using a double 4th (A–D–G) built from the 9th. This adds the 9th to the chord (and does not include the 3rd).

- In measures 9 and 13, Dm7 is voiced by building a major triad from the 3rd: F/D, with octave doubling in measure 13.

- In measures 10 and 14, Em7 is voiced by building a major triad from the 3rd: G/E.

- In measure 16 (and the preceding eighth-note anticipation), Am7 is voiced by building a major triad from the 3rd: C/A.

Our last swing sixteenths groove is in the style of "PCH" (Pacific Coast Highway) by Jeff Lorber, for which we return to a Rhodes-style electric piano sound. This example uses a technique known as "alternating triads" when voicing the minor 7th chords. This involves alternating between two different upper-structure triads in the right hand (built from the 7th and the 3rd), over the same minor 7th chord. This is actually a pop/rock keyboard voicing technique which is also applicable in some funk and smooth jazz situations. On this rhythmically busier groove, note how the left hand plays the root–5th–7th–root pattern in measures 1, 3, 5, and 7, rhythmically fitting in the spaces left by the right-hand part. Elsewhere the left hand is playing roots and 5ths with some rhythmic pickups.

Swing sixteenths groove #3 – Style of "PCH"

TRACK 53
piano only

TRACK 54
piano plus
rhythm section

Swing Sixteenths Groove #3 starts in the key of F minor and transitions into its relative major, A♭, by the end. On the rhythm section track an acoustic guitar is added, doubling some piano voicing top notes in measures 1–8, and playing a simple melody over the comping in measures 9–12. Below are the piano voicings used:

- In measures 1–2 and 5–6, Fm7 is voiced by alternating between major triads built from the 3rd: A♭/F, and from the 7th: E♭/F.

- In measures 3–4 and 7–8, B♭m7 is voiced by alternating between major triads built from the 3rd: D♭/B♭, and from the 7th: A♭/B♭.

- In measure 4, E♭11 is voiced by building a minor triad from the 5th: B♭m/E♭, a variation on building the full minor 7th four-part chord from the 5th: B♭m7/E♭.

- In measure 8, G♭maj7 is voiced by building a minor triad from the 3rd: B♭m/G♭.

- In measures 9 and 11, D♭maj7 is voiced by building a minor triad from the 3rd: Fm/D♭, with an added double 4th embellishment (C–F–B♭, built from the 7th of the chord) in measure 9.

- In measures 9 and 11, E♭11 is voiced by building a minor 7th four-part chord from the 5th: B♭m7/E♭.

- In measure 10, Fm7 is voiced by building a major triad from the 3rd: A♭/F.

- In measure 10, G♭maj9 is voiced by building a minor 7th four-part chord from the 3rd: B♭m7/G♭.

- In measure 12 (and its preceding eighth-note anticipation), A♭maj7 is voiced by building a minor triad from the 3rd: Cm/A♭.

Now that we've worked through a series of comping grooves in smooth jazz styles, it's time to develop some melody and solo techniques for the right hand.

Chapter 5
SMOOTH JAZZ MELODIES and SOLOING

In this chapter we will see how melodies and solos are put together in smooth jazz styles. The keyboardist will normally play the melody or solo in the right hand, supported by chord voicings around the middle C area in the left hand. Most of the upper-structure voicings derived in Chapter 3 will now work as left-hand support voicings in this chapter. As most of these upper structures do not contain the root of the overall chord, they are sometimes referred to as "rootless" voicings when used in the left hand. When playing with a rhythm section, the root of the overall chord would typically be provided by the bass player.

The play-along audio contains two tracks for each melody and solo example. The first track (which is at a slower tempo for the solo examples) has just the piano right hand (the melody or solo part) on the right channel and the piano left-hand voicings plus the rhythm section on the left channel. This enables you to practice the melody or solo using the right hand only by turning down the right channel. The second track has the piano part (left and right hands) on the right channel and the rhythm section on the left channel. This enables you to practice the melody or solo together with the left-hand voicings by turning down the right channel. Of course, you're also encouraged to create your own melody and solo ideas over these progressions when jamming along with the band!

Generally, when distinguishing between melodies and solos, we could say that a melody is a predetermined sequence of notes, whereas a solo is an improvised sequence of notes. In both cases these notes would be supported (or "harmonized") using chord changes. In contemporary styles, we might write a melody and then fit the chords to it, or we might come up with a melody which works over a predetermined chord progression. On the other hand, improvised solos normally occur over an existing progression—often one which has been used to harmonize the main melody of the tune. Regardless of the style, it is still desirable to make our solos as "melodic" as possible so that they are attractive to listen to.

Melodies in smooth jazz styles often consist of short or sparse phrases, which are then repeated or sequenced. The melodies are not busy or elaborate (as in fusion jazz for example). Solos, on the other hand, can have more notes, often using scale patterns and more intense rhythms. The techniques we are about to explore will apply when creating both melodies and solos.

"Target note" and "scale source" concepts

One approach to constructing a melody or solo is to derive a series of "target notes" on a chord progression. A "target note" is a note within a chord which is a desirable landing point for a melody or solo when played over the chord. A series of target notes therefore gives us a framework around which a melody or solo can be developed. Normal target notes in smooth jazz styles are the 3rd, 5th, 7th, or 9th of the chord. For minor or suspended chords, the 11th is also a useful option. One target note per measure is a good starting point, and this may be varied depending on the chord rhythms and/or tempo of the tune. We saw in Chapter 2 that the 5th of a major, minor, or dominant chord can be altered (♭5 or ♯5) and that the 9th of a dominant chord can also be altered (♭9 or ♯9). These altered 5ths and 9ths make particularly good target notes over altered chords, as they have a lot of color and character.

When connecting between target notes with this method, we would normally use notes from a scale source. This might simply be a major or minor scale relating to the overall key of the tune, or (in more sophisticated or "altered" situations) we might choose scale sources on a chord-by-chord basis—more about this later.

Another approach to constructing a melody or solo is to start out with a scale source (derived from the key) that has an inbuilt melodic character and use that to derive the melodic phrases. The most common situations for this in smooth jazz are when we use the minor pentatonic or blues scale built from the tonic of the minor key. Then when we place the resulting melody over the chord progression in the same key (or derive the chord progression, if we are writing a melody before harmonizing it), we can "let the chips fall where they may" in terms of the melody's relationship to the chords. Generally we want the melody to at least not contradict the harmony, and any non-chord tones should be of short duration and/or fall on weak beats of the measure—not on beats 1 or 3 or their anticipations.

When developing each of the following melody and solo examples, we will assess whether the target note approach has been used, and if so the target note chord functions (3rd, 5th, etc.) will be indicated under the top staff. We will also see what scale sources and patterns have been applied.

Melodies using major and minor scales

Our first melody example uses notes of the C major scale over a simple I–IV–V chord progression in C. This melody is created using target notes, which are shown in parentheses. We have the 3rd and the 5th on the Cmaj9 chord, followed by the 7th on the Fmaj9 chord, and so on throughout the example. The left-hand voicings are all four-part upper structures played around the middle C area.

Melody example #1

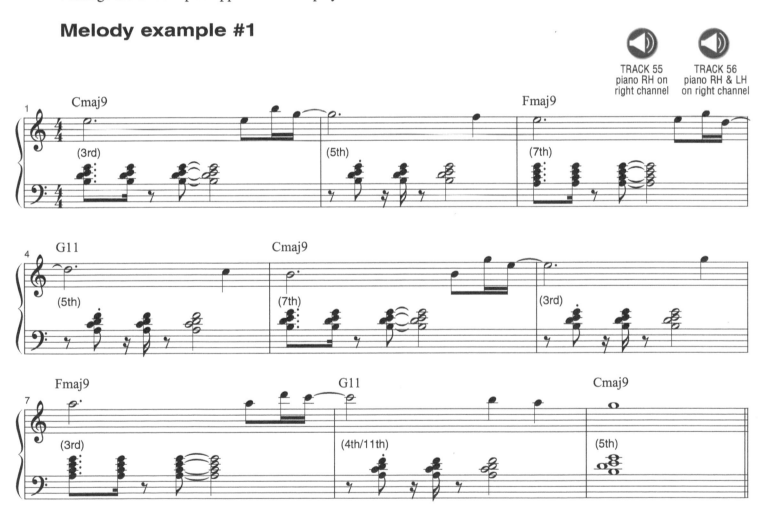

TRACK 55
piano RH on
right channel

TRACK 56
piano RH & LH
on right channel

In between the target notes, other melody notes have been chosen from the C major scale. While there are of course a great many choices of notes and rhythms, we can make the following observations:

• Use of sustained notes at the beginning of the measure, together with the subdivisions and anticipations at the end of the measure, is common in mellow smooth jazz (and new age) melodies.

• Large interval skips in one direction, for instance the E up to B in measure 1, are often followed by smaller intervals in the reverse direction (i.e. the B down to G at the end of the same measure). This is a characteristic of memorable melodies in general.

The left-hand upper-structure voicings of the previous example are all four-part minor 7ths, either built from the 3rds of the major 9th chords (Cmaj9, Fmaj9), or from the 5th of the suspended dominant chord (G11). Here are some practice tips for this last example (which to varying degrees can apply to all the examples in this chapter):

- Play the melody as written to get used to the contour and phrasing.

- Play the target notes as written, and apply your own melodic ideas in between, based on the C major scale. You could start by using the rhythms shown and then introducing your own. (As a warm-up you could also play just the target notes only, if needed).

- Work on choosing your own target notes—again the common choices are the 3rd, 5th, 7th, and 9th of the chords, with the 4th/11th being available instead of the 3rd on the suspended dominant chord (G11). Think about whether you want the sequence of target notes to be ascending, descending, or static, and let that guide your choices accordingly.

- Fill in between your target notes with other scale tones and rhythms as desired—have fun experimenting!

All of the above practice stages can be applied with the right hand only or with both hands, depending on which audio track you use. The next melody example uses notes within the C natural minor scale, over a i–iv–V chord progression in C minor:

Melody example #2

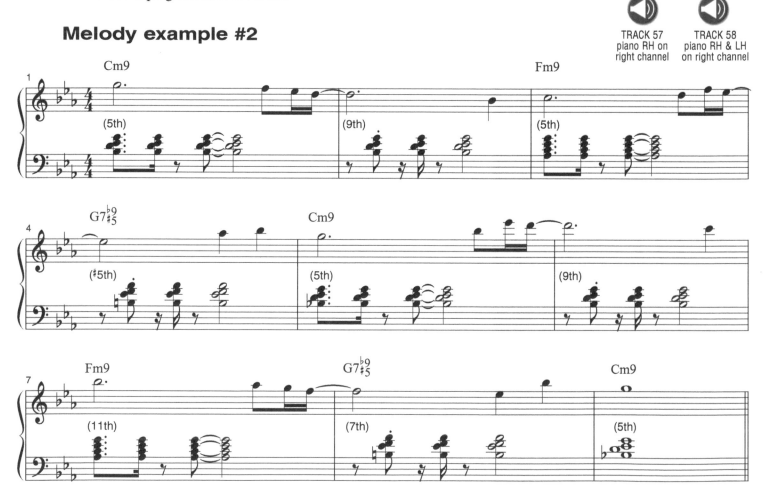

This melody is also created using target notes, which are shown below the top staff. These now include the #5th on the G7♭9#5 chord in measure 4, and the 11th on the Fm9 chord in measure 7. The left-hand upper-structure voicings are all four-part major 7ths built from the 3rds of the minor 9th chords (Cm9, Fm9), except for the four-part m7♭5 built from the 7th of the G7♭9#5 chord. The melodic contour and rhythms are similar to those in Melody Example #1.

Melodies using minor pentatonic and blues scales

Now we will move on to a melody which uses an E minor pentatonic scale over a i–♭VII–v–IV progression in the key of E minor. This melody consists of a repeated motif over different chord changes and was therefore not conceived from a target-note approach. The longer melody notes which "land" on the chord changes do however work on these chords, and so those functions (root, 5th, etc.) are indicated below the top staff. As pentatonic scales consist of whole-step and minor 3rd intervals, simply moving up or down the scale can yield useful and melodic results, as is evident in a lot of smooth jazz and new age music. Note how the ascending or descending pentatonic phrases lead into the sustained melody notes, which fall on eighth-note anticipations.

TRACK 59
piano RH on
right channel

TRACK 60
piano RH & LH
on right channel

Melody example #3

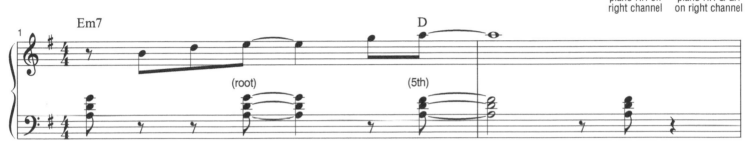

Note the octave runs at the end of measures 4 and 8, punctuating the four-measure phrases. This is a straight-eighths pop-tinged smooth jazz groove with characteristic eighth-note anticipations into each even-numbered measure. The left-hand voicings are a mix of upper-structure double 4ths and triads. The minor 7th chords (Em7, Bm7) are each voiced with a double 4th built from the 4th/11th (inverted on the Bm7), and the major chords are voiced simply with the major triad built from the root.

The next two melody examples both use blues scales. In both cases the blues scale is built from the tonic of a minor key, and the phrases are derived using the inherently strong melodic character of the blues scale, rather than using a target-note concept within the chords. The first example is an up-tempo straight eighths groove in the style of the band the Rippingtons (the long-time smooth jazz vehicle for composer/multi-instrumentalist Russ Freeman) and is in the key of D minor. Note that the sixteen-measure form contains four four-measure phrases using the D blues scale. The first and third phrases are very similar to each other, as are the second and fourth phrases. Also, the melodic phrases do not start right on the first beat of the measure, but instead start on beat 2. These rhythmic and form aspects are all very common in blues-derived smooth jazz melodies.

Melody example #4

TRACK 61
piano RH on
right channel

TRACK 62
piano RH & LH
on right channel

46

Also in the last example we are again using octave runs between the hands, this time every eight measures, derived from the same D blues scale. The left-hand voicings are a mix of upper-structure triads and four-part chords. The minor 7th chords (Dm7, Am7) are each voiced with a major triad built from the 3rd, the minor 9th chords (Gm9) are voiced with a major 7th built from the 3rd, and the major 9th (B♭maj9) and dominant 11th (C11) chords are voiced with minor 7ths built from the 3rd and 5th, respectively.

The next example is in the funkier swing sixteenth style typical of keyboardist/producer Brian Culbertson. This is in the key of F minor and derives its melody from the F blues scale. Note the simple ascending and descending blues scale phrases, using sixteenth-note anticipations.

Melody example #5

TRACK 63
piano RH on
right channel

TRACK 64
piano RH & LH
on right channel

Note the strong rhythmic accents in the left hand, anticipating beat 2 in each measure and beat 4 in the even-numbered measures. The left-hand voicings are all four-part upper structures. The minor 9th chords (Fm9, Gm9) are each voiced with a major 7th built from the 3rd, the major 9th (D♭maj9) and dominant 11th (E♭11) chords are voiced with minor 7ths built from the 3rd and 5th, respectively, and the altered dominant chords (C7♭9♯5) are voiced with m7♭5 chords built from the 7th.

Soloing with blues and pentatonic scales

Now we will move on to some improvised solo examples in smooth jazz styles. The next few examples each emphasize a particular scale source technique: blues, pentatonic, modal, etc. This is done at first to help you focus on these techniques individually. In practice, these ideas can be freely combined together, as we will see in the last solo example in this chapter. If the blues scale is being used to develop a solo, again it is most likely to be related to the key as a whole (rather than changing scales on a chord-by-chord basis). This is what jazz improvisers sometimes refer to as "playing **over** the changes." If however we are developing a solo using other scale source techniques, we might instead be changing scales chord-by-chord, sometimes referred to as "playing **through** the changes." This soloing approach is more likely to use target notes within the chord progression to shape the solo as desired.

The first solo example uses a C blues scale over a slow- to mid-tempo funky straight-sixteenths groove in the key of C minor. The solo phrasing uses a lot of anticipations and "weak sixteenths" (the 2nd and 4th sixteenth notes within a beat), and the blues scale phrases start partway into the measure. The continuous sixteenths (in measures 3–5 and 7–8) would normally be too busy or intense for a smooth jazz melody, but they work fine in the context of a solo. In measures 4, 7, and 8 we use a "drone" (a held and/or repeated note) of C above other notes in the C blues scale, and we use some half-step grace notes leading to the 5th (G). These are all very typical blues phrasing techniques.

Solo example #1

TRACK 65
piano RH
on right
channel—slow

TRACK 66
piano RH & LH
on right channel
—full speed

Although most of the solo phrases in Solo Example #1 use adjacent notes within the blues scale, there are some larger intervals used, particularly in measure 5 where both ascending (G–C–F) and descending (E♭–B♭–F) double 4th shapes are arpeggiated. Using double 4ths in this way is an effective contemporary jazz technique and imparts a modern flavor to the solo. Also note the ascending groups of three notes each in measures 6 and 7 (E♭–F–G, F–G–B♭, G–B♭–C, etc.) using the C minor pentatonic scale. This kind of pentatonic phrase sequencing is widely used in styles ranging from rock to smooth jazz and new age.

The phrase leading into measure 8 is a great example of playing "over the changes"—you might think that the high C would not work over the G+7 chord, particularly as it clashes with the 3rd of the chord (B) in the left-hand voicing. However the unique melodic character of the blues scale allows the ear to forgive these vertical contradictions. For more information on blues scale motifs and phrasing please check out my companion volume in this Keyboard Style Series, *Blues Piano* (also published by Hal Leonard Corporation).

The left-hand voicings used are a mixture of double 4th and four-part upper structures. On the Cm7 chord we are alternating between two double 4ths, built from the 4th/11th and the 5th. The Fm9 chord is voiced with a major 7th built from the 3rd, the Dm7♭5 chord is voiced with a minor triad built from the 3rd, and the G+7 chord is voiced using 7-3 extended (7–3–♯5). Using double 4ths in the left hand around the middle C area is actually a technique pioneered by jazz piano icon Bill Evans in the 1950s, and his voicing style has influenced a legion of piano players to follow, including today's contemporary jazzers.

Note also the rhythms used when playing the left-hand part. Normally the voicing lands on beat 1 of each measure, then one (or occasionally two) more times during the measure. These rhythmic events usually fall on either the second or fourth sixteenth note within the beat (the "weak sixteenths"). For example, in measure 1 the voicing falls on the second sixteenth of beat 3, in measure 2 the second sixteenth of beat 4, in measure 4 the fourth sixteenth of beat 2 (anticipating beat 3), and so on. This imparts a funky or syncopated effect to the groove.

The next solo example uses major pentatonic scale sources on a chord-by-chord basis in conjunction with a target-note approach. This involves building a pentatonic scale from a chord tone (3rd, 5th, 7th) of the chord symbol, in much the same way as we would build an upper-structure voicing. The most common chord/scale relationships for pentatonic scales in smooth jazz (and in pop/rock/R&B) are as follows, with the chord tones in ascending scale sequence in parentheses:

- On major triads or 7th chords, we can build a pentatonic scale from the root (giving us the root, 9th/2nd, 3rd, 5th, and 6th), or from the 5th (giving us the 5th, 6th, 7th, 9th/2nd, and 3rd).

- On minor triads or 7th chords, we can build a pentatonic scale from the 3rd (giving us the 3rd, 11th/4th, 5th, 7th, and root), or from the 7th (giving us the 7th, root, 9th/2nd, 11th/4th, and 5th).

- On suspended dominant 7th chords, we can build a pentatonic scale from the 7th (giving us the 7th, root, 9th/2nd, 11th/4th, and 5th).

We will put these ideas to work in the following example.

Solo example #2 (swing sixteenths)

TRACK 67
piano RH on
right channel
—slow

TRACK 68
piano RH & LH
on right channel
—full speed

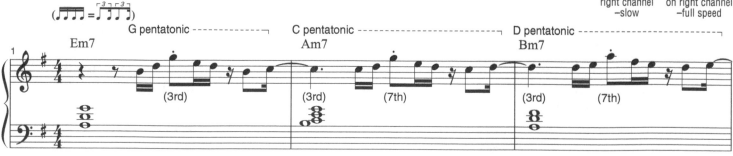

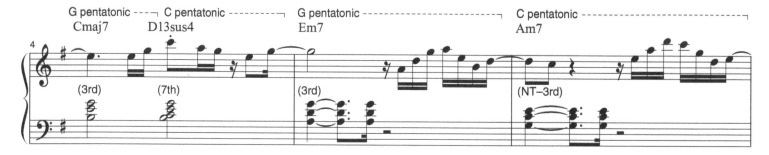

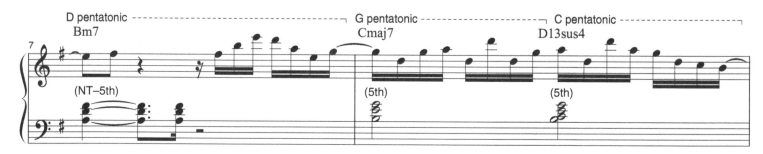

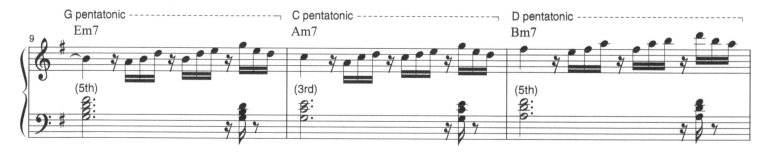

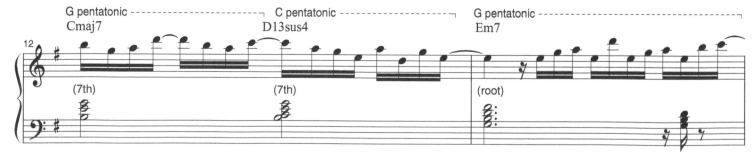

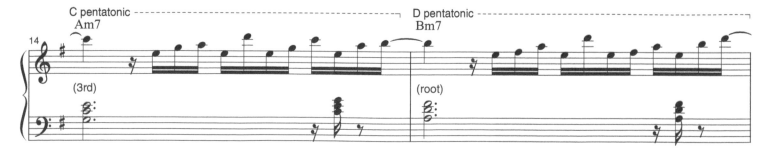

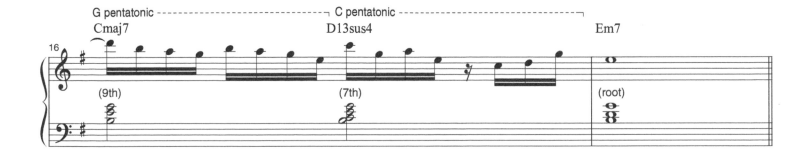

This example is in the key of E minor and has a swing-sixteenths funk feel. Note that phrases from different pentatonic scales (indicated above the treble staff) have been used to connect between the target notes on each chord (indicated between the staves). Pentatonic scales have been built from the 3rds of the minor 7th chords (Em7, Am7, Bm7), from the 5th of the major 7th chord (Cmaj7), and from the 7th of the suspended dominant chord (D13sus4).

The target-note techniques in the above solo example have been further developed with the use of "neighbor tones" (indicated by the letters "NT" between the staves). Instead of landing on the target tone at the point of chord change, we instead land on the neighbor tone and then resolve into the target tone. In this case the neighbor tones are the 11ths of the Am7 and Bm7 chords (in measures 6–7), which resolve to the 3rd and 5th of the chords, respectively.

This example uses some sequencing and repetition of motifs (short melodic phrases) to build longer solo lines. Each four-measure section starts with an initial motif, which is then modified and/or transposed to work within the pentatonic scale restrictions over the following three measures. We are also using ascending and descending double-4th phrases beginning in measure 5 (A–D–G, A–E–B, etc.) and adjacent three-note phrases beginning in measure 9 (A–B–D, B–D–E, etc.). The individual phrases frequently start and/or end on a "weak sixteenth"—common in smooth jazz and funk soloing.

The left-hand voicings used are a mixture of double 4th, triad, and four-part upper structures, some of which upgrade the chord symbols with added extensions. The Em7 chord is voiced with either a double 4th built from the 4th/11th, a major triad built from the 3rd, or a major 7th built from the 3rd. The Am7 chord is voiced with either a major triad built from the 3rd or a major 7th built from the 3rd. The Bm7 chord is voiced with a major triad built from the 3rd. The Cmaj7 chord is voiced with a minor triad built from the 3rd, and the D13sus4 chord is voiced with a major 7th built from the 7th.

Soloing with Dorian and Mixolydian modes

The next solo example also has a swing-sixteenths feel and uses Dorian and Mixolydian modes as scale sources within a target-note framework:

Solo example #3 (swing sixteenths)

TRACK 69
piano RH on
right channel
–slow

TRACK 70
piano RH & LH
on right channel
–full speed

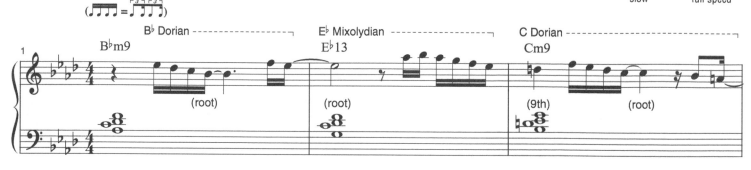

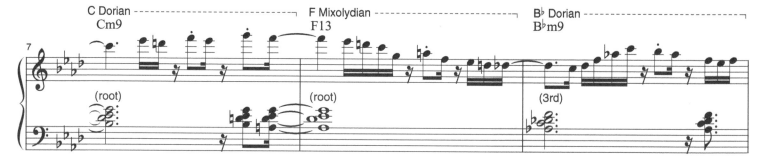

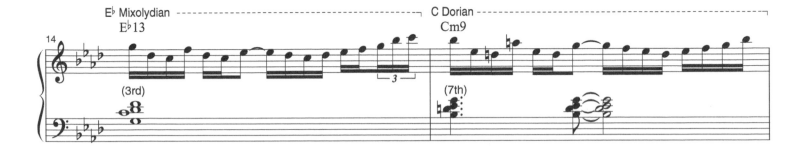

This is a repeating series of ii–V progressions. The B♭m9 and E♭13 chords are a ii–V in A♭ major, and the Cm9 and F13 chords are a ii–V in B♭ major. Therefore, although we are in the key of A♭ according to the key signature, the progression in fact alternates between the "momentary keys" of A♭ and B♭.

The scale sources used are Dorian modes built from the root of the minor 9th chords (B♭m9, Cm9) and Mixolydian modes built from the root of the dominant 13th chords (E♭13, F13). You can think of the dominant 13th chord as a "dominant 9th with added 13th." We saw in Chapter 2 that Dorian and Mixolydian modes are based on major scales but start on the 2nd and 5th degrees, respectively. This means the scale sources for measures 1–2 (B♭ Dorian and E♭ Mixolydian) contain the same notes as the A♭ major scale, and the scale sources for measures 3–4 (C Dorian and F Mixolydian) are the same notes as the B♭ major scale. This alternative way of looking at the scale sources is more "momentary key"-based rather than chord-by-chord.

Motific sequencing and development are used in the solo: the descending four-note groups in measures 1–3, and the ascending 3rds followed by descending 2nds in measures 4–6, etc. Arpeggiated upper-structure four-part chords are also used in measures 9–11, followed by a run of descending 3rds and ascending 2nds using sixteenth-note triplets in measure 12.

The left-hand voicings are all four-part upper structures in second inversion. The minor 9th chords (B♭m9, Cm9) are each voiced with a major 7th built from the 3rd, and the dominant 13th chords (E♭13, F13) are each voiced with a major 7th♭5 built from the 7th: D♭maj7♭5/E♭ and E♭maj7♭5/F.

The next solo example uses the B♭ Dorian mode as a solo scale source throughout over a moderate straight-eighths groove. The progression alternates between B♭m7 and Cm7 chords, which are, respectively, ii and iii in the key of A♭ major. There is not really a target-note concept at work here; rather we are "playing over the changes" using motifs from the B♭ Dorian mode. This creates a "floating" impression characteristic of some modal jazz and new age styles.

Solo example #4

TRACK 71
piano RH
on right
channel—slow

TRACK 72
piano RH & LH
on right channel
—full speed

Intervals were used effectively in this solo part—mostly ascending or descending 2nds (adjacent scale degrees), with some ascending double 4th arpeggios (measures 2, 3, and 8) and descending 3rds (measure 4) mixed in. The left-hand voicings on these minor chords are either double 4ths built from the 4th/11th (inverted), major triads built from the 3rd, or a major 7th built from the 3rd in the case of the last B♭m9 chord.

Soloing with altered scales over dominant chords

The next solo example is a straight-sixteenths groove using more altered harmony and scale sources, in the style of Yellowjackets, Spyro Gyra, and others. The chord progression is a i–VI–II–V vamp in C minor and uses altered dominant chords for the VI, II, and V, which is characteristic of many jazz tunes and turn-arounds. Back in Chapter 2 we derived the melodic minor scale, and now we are going to use it as an altered scale source by building it from the flatted 9th of each altered dominant chord (the flatted 9th is equivalent to a half-step above the root). For example, the A♭ melodic minor scale consists of the notes A♭–B♭–C♭–D♭–E♭–F–G. If we play this scale over a G7, we get (in ascending scale sequence) the ♭9th, ♯9th, 3rd, ♭5th/♯11th, ♯5th/♭13th, 7th, and root of the chord. Jazz improvisers routinely use this scale to spice up or alter dominant chords. Over the I chord (Cm7) the solo uses the C natural minor scale. These scale sources are then used to connect between target notes on each chord.

Solo example #5

TRACK 73
piano RH
on right
channel—slow

TRACK 74
piano RH & LH
on right channel
—full speed

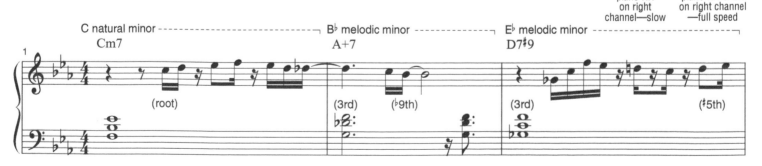

The target notes indicated at the end of measures 3 and 6 of the previous example refer to the chord in the following measure; these notes anticipate beat 1 of the next measure and harmonically "belong" to the following chord. We have used some arpeggiated double 4ths (in measures 3 and 11) and arpeggiated triads and four-part chords (in measures 4, 9, and 17). Note the syncopated rhythms and "weak sixteenths" used when descending within the B♭ and E♭ melodic minor scales in measures 7–8, and the ascending sixteenth-note run in measure 10, which results in a quick change of register for the right hand. Measures 14–16 develop a motif using the same rhythm and overall contour, modifying the notes to fit each of the melodic minor scale sources.

The left-hand voicings are all either double 4ths or 7-3 extended, except for measure 19, where the Cm9 chord is voiced with a major 7th built from the 3rd. Otherwise the Cm7 chords are voiced with double 4ths built from either the 4th/11th or the 5th. The dominant chords are all voiced with 7-3 extended, resulting in (7–3–♯5) on the A+7 and G+7 chords, and (3–7–♯9) on the D7♯9 chords.

Combining all soloing techniques

Our final solo example now combines all of the previous scale source and target-note techniques over a funky swing-sixteenths groove which alternates between the relative keys of E minor and G major. The target notes and scale sources have been indicated.

Solo example #6 (swing sixteenths)

TRACK 75
piano RH
on right
channel—slow

TRACK 76
piano RH & LH
on right channel
—full speed

The target note at the end of measure 9 is an anticipation of the D7#9 chord in the following measure. Scales built from the tonic of the minor key have sometimes been used over chords:

*   The E blues scale is used over Em7 in measures 3 and 5, and over Gmaj9 in measure 13.
*   The E Dorian mode is used over F#m7 in measure 6 and over Em7 in measure 7.

Otherwise the scale sources have been built starting from chord tones on a chord-by-chord basis:

*   The G pentatonic scale has been built from of the 3rd of Em7 in measure 1.
*   The A pentatonic scale has been built from of the 3rd of F#m7 in measure 2.
*   The C melodic minor scale has been built from of the ♭9th of B7#9 in measures 2 and 6.
*   The G pentatonic scale has been built from of the 5th of Cmaj9 in measures 4 and 8.
*   The C pentatonic scale has been built from of the 7th of D11 in measure 4.
*   The D Mixolydian mode has been built from of the root of D11 in measure 8.
*   The D pentatonic scale has been built from of the 5th of Gmaj9 in measures 9, 11, and 15.
*   The E♭ melodic minor scale has been built from of the ♭9th of D7#9 in measures 10, 12, 14, and 16.

The left-hand voicings are a mixture of double 4ths, triads, four-part chords, and 7-3 extended. Have fun playing the solos in this chapter, and then work on creating your own solo ideas by playing them along with the audio tracks—and don't forget to use the slower tempo versions at first, if necessary!

Chapter 6
STYLE FILE

In this chapter we have seven tunes written in different smooth jazz styles. The piano parts for all of the tunes have comping or chordal accompaniment sections as well as melody and/or solo sections. In the comping sections, the right hand is normally playing the upper-structure voicings, as in the Chapter 4 examples. In the melody and solo sections, the left hand is now playing the upper-structure voicings, below the melody or solo in the right hand (as in the Chapter 5 examples).

We will analyze the form of each tune. This involves labeling the different sections of the tune: Intro, A section, B section, Solo, Coda, etc. The intro section (if present) normally establishes the rhythmic groove and style of the tune. The A section occurs when the first melody or theme is introduced. This will often (but not always) use a similar chord progression to the intro. If the tune then transitions into different melody and/or harmony sections, more labels (often called **rehearsal letters**) such as "B section," "C section," etc., can be used. The **solo section** is where an improvised solo occurs (for these tunes, this will be an electric or acoustic piano solo). The solo section typically uses the chord progression from an earlier section of the tune, such as "A" or "B." Finally there may be a separate **coda** which is the end section of the tune.

In many of these tunes, the piano comps through the first A and/or B sections below another instrument playing the melody, such as a synth or guitar. Then when these sections repeat, the piano takes over the melody, sometimes in unison with another instrument. Some of the arrangements also include extra comping instruments (synth pads, clav, etc.) to complement the piano part.

These tunes are all recorded with a band (bass, drums, and comping and melody instruments) as well as piano. On the audio tracks, the band (minus the piano) is on the left channel, and the piano is on the right channel. To play along with the band on these tunes, just turn down the right channel. Slow as well as full speed tracks are provided for each song, except for tune 3, which is already at a slow ballad tempo.

1. Live Inside Your Love

The first tune is written in the style of "How Deep Does It Go," by Carl Anderson. This is a mid-tempo straight-eighths groove in the key of G minor, recorded with an electric piano sound. The intro (measures 1–8) uses sustained chords, with four-part upper structures and some 7-3 extended voicings in the right hand. The first A section (measures 9–24) settles into the main comping groove, rhythmically busier than the intro, with more subdivisions and anticipations. The first B section (measures 25–32) introduces a synth brass melody supported by a more arpeggiated-style piano comping part. During the second A section (measures 33–48), the piano takes over the melody in the right hand supported by left-hand voicings around the middle C area. Then the synth brass doubles the piano melody through the second B section (measures 49–56), into the coda (measures 57–59).

Make sure the intro voicings are smooth and legato, and that the anticipations are articulated clearly once the main groove kicks in. The right-hand melody parts should project dynamically, supported at a lower level by the left-hand voicings.

TRACK 77
slow

TRACK 78
full speed

2. On the Slopes

Next up is a tune written in the style of "Aspen" by the Rippingtons, for whom this type of bright swing-eighths "shuffle" groove is a signature sound. Although this tune is written in the key of F major, the chords in the intro and A sections alternate between suspended dominants built from the tonic (Eb/F) and flatted 7th (Db/Eb) of the key, resulting in extra accidentals (in this case flats) being needed in the notation. Also note that we are using a 12/8 time signature instead of the more typical 4/4. As we saw in Chapter 4, when tunes use a swing-eighths feel, it is sometimes more convenient to notate them in 12/8 time rather than 4/4, if this avoids us having to write a lot of triplet signs in the music.

This example was recorded with a bright acoustic piano sound. The intro (measures 1–4) uses upper-structure triads on beat 1 of each measure and embellishments within these triads in the last half of each measure. In the first A section (measures 5–12) the main shuffle comping groove is established, with the left hand playing staccato pickups in between the right-hand voicings. At this point the piano comping pattern is supporting a synth melody line. In the first B section (measures 13–20) the piano is using some four-part and triad upper structures, with arpeggios leading into beat 3 of each measure. The synth melody tone is changed to an analog synth-brass type sound. During the second A and B sections (measures 21–36), the piano plays an improvised solo in the right hand, supported by the left-hand double 4th and four-part voicings. Finally, the piano comping resumes below the synth melody for the last A section (measures 37–43).

Make sure the right-hand upbeats are crisp and staccato-style in the A sections, contrasting with the more flowing style needed in the B sections. The piano solo uses a mixture of devices and chord/scale relationships that we derived in Chapter 5. After you have worked through this, see if you can improvise your own solo over the chord changes!

TRACK 79
slow

TRACK 80
full speed

3. Sweetest Dreams

Our next example is a straight-sixteenths ballad in the style of "Just to Be Loved" by Al Jarreau, whose R&B/pop-influenced jazz is a staple of smooth jazz radio playlists. This example is in the key of E♭ major and was recorded using a Rhodes-style electric piano sound. Note that the main A section is built around a iii–VI–ii–V–I progression using altered dominant chords. This is a common harmonic structure across the spectrum of jazz styles.

The tune starts with a double A section (measures 1–16) which establishes the right-hand comping rhythm used for most of the tune, using a mix of triad, double 4th, and four-part upper-structure voicings. In the first B section (measures 17–24) a string synth melody enters, supported by the piano comping. During the second double A and single B sections (measures 25–48), the piano takes over the melody in the right hand, supported by the left-hand double 4th and four-part voicings. The piano then continues playing the melody during the coda (measures 49–53).

When comping, make sure the left-hand pickups (on the second sixteenth of beat 1 and halfway through beat 3) lead smoothly into the right-hand voicings. When playing the melody, make sure the right-hand part projects over the left-hand voicings.

TRACK 81
full speed

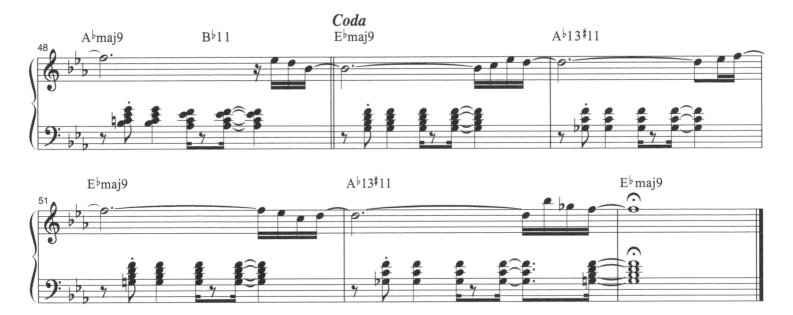

4. Jacket and Tie

The next example is a more uptempo straight-sixteenths groove in the style of "Homecoming" by the Yellowjackets. The overall intensity and innovation of this band's music would put them more into the "contemporary jazz" or "jazz fusion" category; however some of their more commercial output also works as smooth jazz. This example is in the key of G major and was recorded with an acoustic piano sound.

The tune starts with an A section (measures 1–16) using a mix of double-4th inversions and triad upper structures in the right hand, also creating a top note melody with the highest notes of these voicings using eighth- and sixteenth-note anticipations. This is accompanied on the audio track by a sixteenth-note arpeggiated synth pattern, which is a signature Yellowjackets device. In the first B section (measures 17–26) a synth melody enters, doubled by the top notes of the piano voicings at this point. During the second A section (measures 27–42), the piano then plays the melody as single notes in the right hand, supported by left-hand double 4th inversions and four-part voicings. Here the piano melody is doubled with another synth sound. During the second B section (measures 43–57), the piano plays an improvised solo in the right hand, supported by left-hand double-4th, triad, and four-part voicings.

Note the modern, transparent sound of this example, mainly due to the double-4th voicings and inversions. Although use of the sustain pedal is recommended for the first A and B sections, I would suggest not using it during the solo section (that is, over the second B section), as it can detract from the articulation and clarity of the solo phrasing. That being the case, you should try to hold the left-hand voicings down for as long as you can during this section, as the sustain pedal is not there to help you. After playing through this solo, use it as a springboard for your own improvisation ideas!

TRACK 82
slow

TRACK 83
full speed

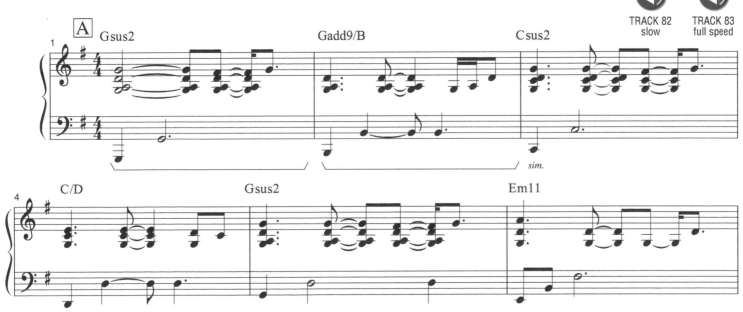

5. Listen to Me

Our next piece is another straight-sixteenths groove in the style of "See What I'm Sayin'" by Boney James. This example features some busier chord rhythms (two or more chords per measure), less common phrase lengths (the ten-measure A section consists of two five-measure phrases), and some 2/4 measures in addition to the normal 4/4. This piece alternates between the relative keys of C minor and E♭ major and was recorded using an electric piano sound.

The tune starts with an A section (measures 1–10), with both hands playing the same sixteenth-note rhythm and anticipating beat 3 of each 4/4 measure. The right hand is mostly playing upper-structure triads, with some four-part and 7-3 extended voicings. During the second five-measure phrase in the first A section, an acoustic guitar melody is added over the piano comping part. In the first B section (measures 11–18), the left and right hands continue playing simultaneous rhythms, now using more four-part upper-structure voicings, and a synth melody is added. During the second A section (measures 19–27) the main rhythm section groove kicks in, and the piano comping becomes a little busier with some left-hand pickups. At this point a resonant synth clav is added to complement the piano part. This A section is truncated (just nine measures) in order to lead into the solo section (measures 28–39). Here the piano is playing an improvised solo using the F Dorian mode, "playing over" the repeated changes of Fm7 and Gm7, supported by left-hand four-part voicings. The last A section (measures 40–48) then returns to the main groove and melody of the tune.

Ensure that you articulate the simultaneous sixteenth-note rhythms cleanly and evenly with both hands, observing the rests and anticipations. Watch out for the 2/4 measures, and keep track of the form (the number of measures in each section). Make sure you have the F Dorian mode comfortably under your fingers, and then work on your own modal improvisation in the solo section!

TRACK 84 slow   TRACK 85 full speed

6. Gotta Groove

Next up is a funky swing-sixteenths groove in the style of "Get It On" by Brian Culbertson. The rhythm section track has a synthesized feel typical for this artist, and this together with the acoustic piano creates a useful timbral combination for some of the more electronically-inclined smooth jazzers. This example is in the key of C minor, briefly implying the relative major of E♭ in the B section.

The tune starts with an intro (measures 1–8) which establishes the piano comping pattern, with the rhythm section groove entering in measure 5. The right hand is playing a mix of upper-structure triads, four-part, and 7-3 extended voicings. In the first A section (measures 9–16) the piano plays the melody, which is derived from the C blues scale. At this point there is no left-hand comping—we just have a string synth and rhythm section on the backing track. In the first B section (measures 17–20, functioning as a "build" or "set-up" into the C section), we resume the two-handed piano comping with a top-note melody that's doubled by a synth. Then in the first C section (measures 21–28), the piano uses an "alternating triad" upper-structure pattern (this time doubled by an analog brass synth), and a sparse synth countermelody is added on top. During the second A section (measures 29–36), the piano is playing a similar two-handed comping pattern to the intro, and the original A section melody is now given to a synth. In the second B section (measures 37–40), the piano doubles the melody in the right hand, above four-part voicings used in the left hand. Finally, the second C section (measures 41–48) is a repeat of the first, ending the tune on an octave phrase derived from the C minor pentatonic scale.

Some of the piano comping here is a little more dense or complex (particularly in the C section); practice this at a slow tempo and/or with hands separately, as needed. Keep the anticipations "crisp" and observe the rests in these comping sections. Also feel free to experiment with your own melody ideas over the first A section, as described above.

TRACK 86
slow

TRACK 87
full speed

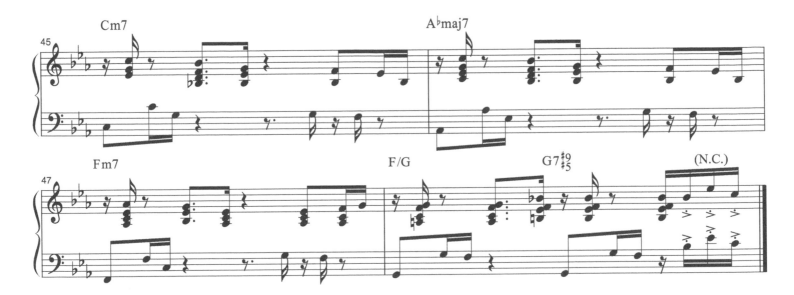

7. Night Games

Our last tune is another swing-sixteenths groove, this time in the more mellow style of "88 Ways to Love" by Marcus Johnson. This example moves between the relative keys of B minor and D major. Again we are using the popular combination of acoustic piano melody with synthesized/electronic rhythm section, this time including some electric piano comping. If you are playing an electronic keyboard with "split" capability (the ability to play two different sounds on either side of a "split point"), then assign an acoustic piano from the A right above middle C upwards, and an electric piano from the G♯ above middle C downwards. That way you will be able to play the melody using acoustic piano and comp using electric piano, which is how the track was recorded. However, don't worry if you can't do this on your keyboard—you'll still be able to play along with the track with whatever piano sound you have available.

The tune starts with an intro (measures 1–8), during which the right hand plays some sparse acoustic piano fills derived from the B natural minor scale. In the first A section (measures 9–16), the electric piano plays rhythmically simple half- and whole-note chords, using triad and four-part upper-structure voicings. At this point a synth melody is added above the piano comping. In the B section the electric piano comping gets a little busier, with some arpeggiation of the upper structures towards the end of each measure and some root-5th and root-7th intervals added in the left hand. In the second A and B sections (measures 25–40) both hands are playing on either side of the split point, with the right hand playing the acoustic piano melody, and the left hand comping mostly triads and four-part upper structures on the electric piano around the middle C area. In the coda (measures 41–49), the right hand repeats the acoustic piano fills from the intro, this time supported by the electric piano comping in the left hand.

When you're comfortable with the groove, go ahead and experiment with your own piano fills in the intro and coda sections, as well as the piano melody in the second A section. Enjoy!

TRACK 88 slow   TRACK 89 full speed

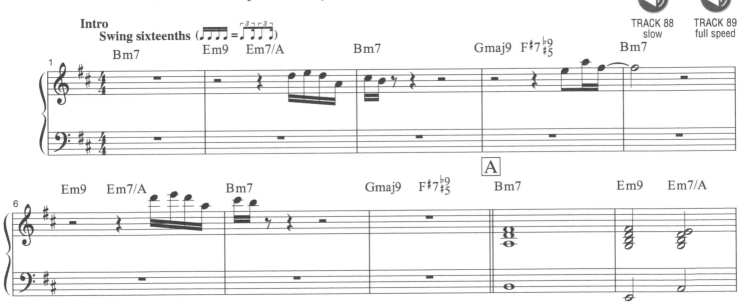

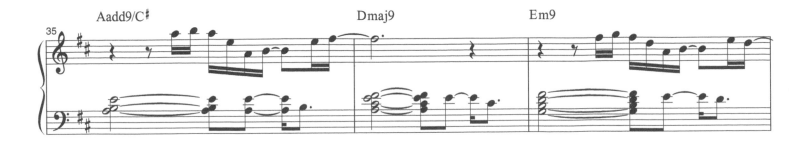

KEYBOARD STYLE SERIES

THE COMPLETE GUIDE!

These book/audio packs provide focused lessons that contain valuable how-to insight, essential playing tips, and beneficial information for all players. From comping to soloing, comprehensive treatment is given to each subject. The companion audio features many of the examples in the book performed either solo or with a full band.

BEBOP JAZZ PIANO
by John Valerio
This book provides detailed information for bebop and jazz keyboardists on: chords and voicings, harmony and chord progressions, scales and tonality, common melodic figures and patterns, comping, characteristic tunes, the styles of Bud Powell and Thelonious Monk, and more.
00290535 Book/Online Audio $18.99

BEGINNING ROCK KEYBOARD
by Mark Harrison
This comprehensive book/audio package will teach you the basic skills needed to play beginning rock keyboard. From comping to soloing, you'll learn the theory, the tools, and the techniques used by the pros. The accompanying audio demonstrates most of the music examples in the book.
00311922 Book/Online Audio $14.99

BLUES PIANO
by Mark Harrison
With this book/audio pack, you'll learn the theory, the tools, and even the tricks that the pros use to play the blues. Covers: scales and chords; left-hand patterns; walking bass; endings and turnarounds; right-hand techniques; how to solo with blues scales; crossover licks; and more.
00311007 Book/Online Audio $19.99

BOOGIE-WOOGIE PIANO
by Todd Lowry
From learning the basic chord progressions to inventing your own melodic riffs, you'll learn the theory, tools and techniques used by the genre's best practicioners.
00117067 Book/Online Audio $17.99

BRAZILIAN PIANO
by Robert Willey and Alfredo Cardim
Brazilian Piano teaches elements of some of the most appealing Brazilian musical styles: choro, samba, and bossa nova. It starts with rhythmic training to develop the fundamental groove of Brazilian music.
00311469 Book/Online Audio $19.99

CONTEMPORARY JAZZ PIANO
by Mark Harrison
From comping to soloing, you'll learn the theory, the tools, and the techniques used by the pros. The full band tracks on the audio feature the rhythm section on the left channel and the piano on the right channel, so that you can play along with the band.
00311848 Book/Online Audio $18.99

COUNTRY PIANO
by Mark Harrison
Learn the theory, the tools, and the tricks used by the pros to get that authentic country sound. This book/audio pack covers: scales and chords, walkup and walkdown patterns, comping in traditional and modern country, Nashville "fretted piano" techniques and more.
00311052 Book/Online Audio $19.99

GOSPEL PIANO
by Kurt Cowling
Discover the tools you need to play in a variety of authentic gospel styles, through a study of rhythmic devices, grooves, melodic and harmonic techniques, and formal design. The accompanying audio features over 90 tracks, including piano examples as well as the full gospel band.
00311327 Book/Online Adio $17.99

INTRO TO JAZZ PIANO
by Mark Harrison
From comping to soloing, you'll learn the theory, the tools, and the techniques used by the pros. The accompanying audio demonstrates most of the music examples in the book. The full band tracks feature the rhythm section on the left channel and the piano on the right channel, so that you can play along with the band.
00312088 Book/Online Audio $17.99

JAZZ-BLUES PIANO
by Mark Harrison
This comprehensive book will teach you the basic skills needed to play jazz-blues piano. Topics covered include: scales and chords • harmony and voicings • progressions and comping • melodies and soloing • characteristic stylings.
00311243 Book/Online Audio $17.99

JAZZ-ROCK KEYBOARD
by T. Lavitz
Learn what goes into mixing the power and drive of rock music with the artistic elements of jazz improvisation in this comprehensive book and CD package. This instructional tool delves into scales and modes, and how they can be used with various chord progressions to develop the best in soloing chops.
00290536 Book/CD Pack..$17.95

LATIN JAZZ PIANO
by John Valerio
This book is divided into three sections. The first covers Afro-Cuban (Afro-Caribbean) jazz, the second section deals with Brazilian influenced jazz – Bossa Nova and Samba, and the third contains lead sheets of the tunes and instructions for the play-along audio.
00311345 Book/Online Audio $17.99

MODERN POP KEYBOARD
by Mark Harrison
From chordal comping to arpeggios and ostinatos, from grand piano to synth pads, you'll learn the theory, the tools, and the techniques used by the pros. The online audio demonstrates most of the music examples in the book.
00146596 Book/Online Audio $17.99

NEW AGE PIANO
by Todd Lowry
From melodic development to chord progressions to left-hand accompaniment patterns, you'll learn the theory, the tools and the techniques used by the pros. The accompanying 96-track CD demonstrates most of the music examples in the book.
00117322 Book/CD Pack..$16.99

POST-BOP JAZZ PIANO
by John Valerio
This book/audio pack will teach you the basic skills needed to play post-bop jazz piano. Learn the theory, the tools, and the tricks used by the pros to play in the style of Bill Evans, Thelonious Monk, Herbie Hancock, McCoy Tyner, Chick Corea and others. Topics covered include: chord voicings, scales and tonality, modality, and more.
00311005 Book/Online Audio $17.99

PROGRESSIVE ROCK KEYBOARD
by Dan Maske
You'll learn how soloing techniques, form, rhythmic and metrical devices, harmony, and counterpoint all come together to make this style of rock the unique and exciting genre it is.
00311307 Book/Online Audio $19.99

R&B KEYBOARD
by Mark Harrison
From soul to funk to disco to pop, you'll learn the theory, the tools, and the tricks used by the pros with this book/audio pack. Topics covered include: scales and chords, harmony and voicings, progressions and comping, rhythmic concepts, characteristic stylings, the development of R&B, and more! Includes seven songs.
00310881 Book/Online Audio $19.99

ROCK KEYBOARD
by Scott Miller
Learn to comp or solo in any of your favorite rock styles. Listen to the audio to hear your parts fit in with the total groove of the band. Includes 99 tracks! Covers: classic rock, pop/rock, blues rock, Southern rock, hard rock, progressive rock, alternative rock and heavy metal.
00310823 Book/Online Audio $17.99

ROCK 'N' ROLL PIANO
by Andy Vinter
Take your place alongside Fats Domino, Jerry Lee Lewis, Little Richard, and other legendary players of the '50s and '60s! This book/audio pack covers: left-hand patterns; basic rock 'n' roll progressions; right-hand techniques; straight eighths vs. swing eighths; glisses, crushed notes, rolls, note clusters and more. Includes six complete tunes.
00310912 Book/Online Audio $18.99

SALSA PIANO
by Hector Martignon
From traditional Cuban music to the more modern Puerto Rican and New York styles, you'll learn the all-important rhythmic patterns of salsa and how to apply them to the piano. The book provides historical, geographical and cultural background info, and the 50+-tracks includes piano examples and a full salsa band percussion section.
00311049 Book/Online Audio $19.99

SMOOTH JAZZ PIANO
by Mark Harrison
Learn the skills you need to play smooth jazz piano – the theory, the tools, and the tricks used by the pros. Topics covered include: scales and chords; harmony and voicings; progressions and comping; rhythmic concepts; melodies and soloing; characteristic stylings; discussions on jazz evolution.
00311095 Book/Online Audio $19.99

STRIDE & SWING PIANO
by John Valerio
Learn the styles of the stride and swing piano masters, such as Scott Joplin, Jimmy Yancey, Pete Johnson, Jelly Roll Morton, James P. Johnson, Fats Waller, Teddy Wilson, and Art Tatum. This book/audio pack covers classic ragtime, early blues and boogie woogie, New Orleans jazz and more. Includes 14 songs.
00310882 Book/Online Audio $19.99

WORSHIP PIANO
by Bob Kauflin
From chord inversions to color tones, from rhythmic patterns to the Nashville Numbering System, you'll learn the tools and techniques needed to play piano or keyboard in a modern worship setting.
00311425 Book/Online Audio $17.99

HAL•LEONARD®

Prices, contents, and availability
subject to change without notice.

www.halleonard.com